How The Beats Begat The Pranksters

& Other Adventure Tales

Merry Prankster's Praise for
The Hitchhiker's Guide to Jack Kerouac

"This is an excellent book about Uncle Jack, and also a heartfelt outpouring of love for Mom and Dad, and the Grateful Dead, too. I just got done reading the section about Mom. Very touching — made me miss her. Thank you for writing this."

Jami Cassady
(Neal & Carolyn's youngest daughter, and "Jack's favorite")

"I'm reading your book and enjoying it immensely. Surprised and enlightened. I'm still laughing from what I read last night. Laughter is the best medicine, and you gave me some big howls. The repartee is so well rendered, and your Ken Babbs descriptions are right on. And very funny. The general mayhem aspect is also spot on. Thanks for the rerun! I was there for part of it with Barlow. Congratulations on creating an awesome read. And thanks for the blast of light! You rock!"

Mountain Girl
(Carolyn Garcia)

"If you have read Kerouac, and are interested in his life and work, and the movement he and his friends inspired, and the effect it has had on our lives since, I suggest reading Brian's fine book. If you have not read Kerouac, I suggest you do so."

George Walker
(Hardly Visible)

"All the details were perfectly right on — which is so rare and admirable — and appreciated by people like me who are irritated by mistakes. Almost universally writers get one thing or another 'off' or backwards or off to one side. I'll put a book down if I find one or more — but I read yours non-stop right to the end as soon as I started it. It was quite the book!"

Roy Sebern
(original Merry Prankster who first painted "Furthur" on the front of The Bus)

"This is good stuff."

Zane Kesey
(son of Ken & Faye)

Other Praise for The Author

"Your article sent me into raptures. I just LOVE the way you write. Your wit and turns of phrase and insights are so unique and beyond compare. You must write many books!"

Carolyn Cassady
(wife of Neal and love of Jack's life)

"Jack would've *loved* you!"

Edie Kerouac Parker
(Jack's first wife)

"This is an exceptionally fine piece of work on your part. Marvelous dissertations and mightily written rapportage!"

Henri Cru
(Remi Boncoeur in *On The Road*)

"I like your distinctive narrative voice. You are a great stylist."

Sterling Lord
(Kerouac & Kesey's literary agent)

"Hombre, let me say right off – you are a hell of a writer! This piece you wrote is just wonderful. I love it! It felt like I was there.....what a treat."

Walter Salles
(director of *On The Road*)

"You're not an *On The Road* scholar — you're an *On The Road* character!"

Teri McLuhan
(Marshall McLuhan's author/filmmaker daughter)

"You can write your ass off!!"

David Amram
(Kerouac's principal musical collaborator)

"If it's happiness you want, Brian Hassett seems to have found it."

Bill Sass
(Edmonton Journal)

How The Beats Begat The Pranksters

and Other Adventure Tales

by
Brian Hassett

Gets Things Done Publishing

ISBN: 978-0-9947262-1-6

First Edition — Sept. 2017 – the Jack & Neal Ride Again Tour
                          100 copy print run
Second Edition — Nov. 2017

Front cover photo of Ken Kesey, Allen Ginsberg & George Walker by Brian Hassett, taken as they were about to drive away on the closing day of the On The Road Jack Kerouac Conference, Sunday, August 1, 1982, in Chautauqua Park, Boulder, Colorado.

Cover design and production by the Michelangelo of books — David Wills.

The book's large 12-point font and open space is intentional.
Books should be fun and easy to read and not a chore.
You're welcome.

For more information and to stay up to date go to . . .

BrianHassett.com

or email — **karmacoupon@gmail.com**

I went away one weekend to a family reunion —
and came away with a stage partner.

I went away the next month to do a show in San
Francisco during the Summer of Love and came
away with a life partner.

This book is dedicated to them.

Sky and George

Contents

Introduction by George Walker i

1. How The Beats Begat The Pranksters 1

2. Lowell Celebrates Kerouac 25

3. Shindig Sutra 29

4. Getting My Phil at the Crossroads 53

5. Then Along Comes Kesey 63

6. On the Road to On the Road 69

7. Making Better Time On the Road 81

8. On the Road Comes Home 101

9. Woodstock with the Pranksters 119

10. Pranksters in Wonderland 135

11. The George & Brian Story 143

12. Keeping the Beat, by George Walker 149

13. I Pick *Pic* 159

14. Be The Invincible Spirit You Are 165

Introduction
by
George "Hardly Visible" Walker

In the summer of 1982, Ken Kesey, Ken Babbs, and I took a road trip to Boulder, Colorado, to attend a Naropa Institute conference celebrating the Beat literature movement and commemorating the 25th anniversary of the publication of *On The Road,* Jack Kerouac's landmark novel that defined the Beat Generation, and inspired so many young Americans to seek a higher level of intellectual and social freedom.

Among those we met there was a young Canadian, Brian Hassett, who had hitchhiked from Vancouver, B. C., and subsequently to Kesey's farm in Oregon, and then, years later, wrote of his adventure in his wonderful book, *The Hitchhiker's Guide to Jack Kerouac.* I didn't see Brian again until 2016, but had followed his exploits through the internet and social media, and knew he was very involved in studying, and furthering the awareness of, Beat literature and the surrounding culture.

What I did not know about was his prowess as a performer, reading both Kerouac and his own writings celebrating the Beats. When I saw him perform his "Beat Café" show at an event called "The Twanger Plunker's Family Reunion" in Indiana, which celebrates the Merry Pranksters, I was floored! He was amazing, bringing a level of energy and enthusiasm to reading that is seldom seen. He brought Kerouac to life in a manner that promised new possibilities.

After his show, we talked, and I told him I could read Neal Cassady ("Dean Moriarty" in *On The Road*) on a level that I believed could complement his Kerouac reading. We agreed to try it, and the next day, after a brief cold-read run-through, I joined him on stage and we read a dialog piece from *On The Road,* Brian reading the Jack part and I reading the Neal part. It went well. The reading was a minor sensation, and we have continued doing our Jack & Neal shows, expanding to more dialog bits with some improvisation.

As enthusiasm for our endeavor built, we became ever more aware of the strong connection between the Beats and the Merry Pranksters, a connection that was cemented early on when Cassady signed on to drive Kesey's "Furthur" bus on our epic journey to New York in 1964, and then became an integral part of the Pranksters, as noted by Tom Wolfe in *The Electric Kool-Aid Acid Test.*

While planning our next tour of "Brian & George read Jack & Neal," Brian hit on the idea of writing an essay, which quickly became this book, *How the Beats Begat The Pranksters,* and he began soliciting input from surviving Pranksters and others who were around who had experiences or knowledge of how this phenomenon had transpired.

The following story is the result of those efforts, and reflects how our culture has grown through the decades since Kerouac wrote his first words and Cassady stole his first car, and how our current Merry Prankster movement traces its roots to those events. Today it is difficult for me to imagine the Pranksters existing without the earlier work of the Beats: Kerouac, the Cassadys, Allen Ginsberg, William Burroughs, John Clellon Holmes, and all the rest who helped define what was cool, and taught us how to look for it.

How The Beats Begat
The Pranksters

It all started on September 5th, 1957 when a certain book got published . . .

Or no . . . it all started in April 1951 when a guy sat down at a typewriter with a long scroll of paper so he didn't have to stop writing every 11 inches . . .

Or no it all started when Neal Cassady came to New York, Christmastime 1946 . . .

Which really flips back to Denver's Hal Chase coming to Columbia University and telling all his new soon-to-be-Beat writer friends about this catalytic conman he knew from Colorado . . .

Which waves back to Twain's playful Huck or Shakespeare's pranksterish Puck or eternity's Irish luck . . .

But what I can tell you for sure is this — pretty much all the Merry Pranksters — from their Perry Lane / Stanford writers' birthplace to the Bus-painting bohos at Ken Kesey's house in La Honda — had read Jack Kerouac's *On The Road* . . . before collectively taking their own Road trip with the real life Dean Moriarty hero of the book, Neal Cassady.

As Kesey used to say when asked how someone becomes a Prankster — "We just recognize each other." And one of the traits — one of those recognizable admission requirements — was that you'd read *On The Road*.

As Kerouac & Grateful Dead scholar Dennis McNally opens the Cassady/Acid Test chapter in his definitive book on the Dead et al, *A Long Strange Trip*, "Neal Leon Cassady was 'Dean Moriarty' in *On The Road*, a fundamental document of the cultural odyssey that all the members of the Grateful Dead would travel."

They had also all heard of Allen Ginsberg's *Howl* because of the internationally reported-on obscenity trial in 1957 that was extra prominent in the local West Coast newspapers, although not many of them had actually read the book, and none of them cited it as a breakthrough work for them. But it sure made everybody aware there was some chit goin on.

Nowadays there are over 50 Kerouac-written books in print, and gawd-knows how many biographies ... and Allen books ... and books by members of the Beat Generation who were barely known of in the late '50s and early '60s. But back then there was really only one book.

It's hard for us in the present to imagine a world with only one Beatles record — but effectively that's what it was for pretty much all the original gelling Pranksters and Dead. It wasn't "Beat" like we know it now — not a group show at the Whitney or de Young, or the latest hardcover collection, or multiple major motion pictures. It was one book. Even though by the early '60s, *The Dharma Bums*, *The Subterraneans*, *Big Sur* and more were in print, not one of the living Pranksters has ever mentioned to me any one of them being read in their pre-Bus-trip years. It was an *On The Road* mindset that changed everything. It was a way people were beginning to think. "It wasn't a club, it was a way of seeing," as Prankster bandleader Jerry Garcia phrased what "Beat" meant to him.

As **Kesey** put it in his essay on Jack for *Esquire*

magazine's "The 50 Who Made The Difference" tribute issue in 1983 — "*On The Road*. Good ol' nation-shaking feet-stirring *On The Road*. What can we call to mind that was like unto it, impact-wise? I can't recall its equal in politics, or art ... not even in music."

Allen Ginsberg and Ken Kesey on stage at the On The Road Kerouac Conference in Boulder in 1982

Speaking of that essay on *Late Night with David Letterman*, he said, "I judge art by how it makes you feel. You go to a movie and if you don't feel better about people when you come out of the movie then, y'know .... done. Art, if it doesn't lift you up, as a human being — and Kerouac, everything you ever read by him, he only puts himself down, and it left everybody that read *On The Road* feeling a lot better about the American scene, the American people. Everybody who read that book for the first time got in the car and immediately headed off across the country and got loaded and loved everybody, and that's canonization business. He's as good as Mother Theresa in his own league."

As he told his official biographer **Robert (Bob) Faggen** in his *Paris Review* interview in 1994, "Many of us had read Ginsberg's *Howl*, Kerouac's *On the Road*, Kenneth Rexroth's work, and Ferlinghetti's. I knew their work when I was a student at the University of Oregon."

3

He was so struck by all that was happening in North Beach that he wrote an early (still unpublished) novel, *Zoo*, entirely set there.

Or as he's quoted in the *Magic Trip* movie, "Everybody I knew read *On The Road* and it opened up doors for us just the same way drugs did. It gave us a new way to look at America, and it stirred us up."

In an unpublished interview with Faggen in 1992, he said, "(I) had read it [*On The Road*] three times before [the '64 Bus trip], hoping to sign on in some way, to join that joyous voyage, like thousands of other volunteers inspired by the same book and its vision."

Speaking with American lit scholar Faggen myself recently, he confirmed, "There's an improvisational spontaneity that Kerouac introduced into American fiction that wasn't there before him."

And speaking of form-stretching improvisational artists, as one **Jerry Garcia** put it, "I read *On The Road* and fell in love with it, the adventure, the romance of it, everything. I owe a lot of who I am and what I've been and what I've done to the Beats from the '50s. I feel like I'm part of a continuous line of a certain thing in American culture, of a root ... I can't imagine myself without that — it's what's been great about the human race and gives you a sense of how great you might get, how far you can reach. And I think the rest of the guys in the band all share stuff like that. We all have those things, those pillars of greatness to lean on. If you're lucky, you find out about them, and if you're not lucky, you don't. And in this day and age in America, a lot of people aren't lucky, and they don't find out about these things."

And another time Jerry said, "I can't separate who I am now from what I got from Kerouac. I don't know if I would ever have had the courage or the vision to do something outside with my life — or even suspected the possibilities existed — if it weren't for Kerouac opening those doors."

Jerry's wife **Mountain Girl** signs copies of *On The Road* with "READ THIS BOOK!" She shared with me that when there was the white-hot spotlight and criticism of the Pranksters and the Dead, Kesey would sometimes tell his challengers with a twinkle that it was the Beats who were to blame for all this.

For a specific example of the Pranksters' ode to what they owed to the Beats and how there was "an unbroken continuum" as she put it, she reminded me that Kesey put together two massive poets/writers summits in the mid-'70s at the University of Oregon with the afterparties on his farm called **"The Poetic Hoohaw"** featuring Ginsberg, Burroughs, Corso, Orlovsky, Bob Kaufman, Jack Micheline, Anne Waldman, all merging on stage with the Prankster wing including Ken Babbs, Wavy Gravy, Paul Krassner, the Flying Karamazov Brothers, and many others.

"The Beats were the ones that poked the big hole into the proprieties of society in the '50s," she riffed. "Back then, what was proper and what was not proper was a huge deal. And the Beats were definitely improper. They weren't proper *at all*," she says with a bursting laugh at the immensity of it all.

Mountain Girl, originally Carolyn Adams, is a living embodiment of the-Beats-begat-the-Pranksters — since she was picked up hitchhiking by none other than Neal Cassady (!) who proceeded to drive her to Ken Kesey's place in La Honda. (!) The car came by, and she got in, that's when it all began. She literally went On The Road with a Beat . . . *to* the Pranksters. She was 18 at the time, 1964, and an early harbinger of the searching questing youth that was about to explode big-time all across America.

She also went from being Kesey's girlfriend to Garcia's wife. "Jerry had a big crush on Kerouac. He loved him," she told me recently. "Neal talked about him endlessly. All the guys in the band had been primed forever with Neal's tales of Jack and Ginsberg. We were all ready to meet these people by the time Neal got done with all his instructions. He was seriously trying to bring people along into his life story. And Jack was a big piece of it. He was *extremely* proud of his relationship with Jack, even though it was troubled. He was very serious about making sure all these young whippersnappers heard the truth. So let's blame Neal," she said, to a duet of laughter.

The Dead's main lyricist, **Robert Hunter**, who actually met Cassady before Kesey did at a communal house nicknamed "The Chateau" near Perry Lane, said of Cassady, "He was flying circles above me. He used to visit me a lot. He paid me the compliment of saying that when he goes to New York, he visits Bill Burroughs, and when he comes here, he hangs at my house.

"He was Mr. Natural for us. He would say things and, if you had him on tape and could listen back, you could hear replies you hadn't heard before — multifaceted replies. The man was phenomenal, a phenomenal brain. Yeah, he was a *wonderful* guy.

"It was hard *not* to be Neal after he was around. He was such a master of any social situation that you'd learn it yourself, and when he was away it would take weeks before you'd stop being Neal. This was true of all of us. He was *such* an original. He had such a dynamic life and it was just *packed*. He enjoyed the *hell* out of it."

Of the music in Jack's writing, Hunter said — "That's bop!" And he later put his voice where his heart was and read Jack as part of both the *Kicks Joy Darkness* CD, and was the voice of Dr. Sax on the audio recording of Kerouac's play *Doctor Sax and The Great World Snake*.

As Babbs put it of the Dead–Prankster connection, "We always thought of the Grateful Dead as being the engine that was driving the spaceship we were traveling on."

In his excellent memoir, *Searching For The Sound*, Dead bassist **Phil Lesh** wrote, "Neal was the closest thing to poetry in motion I've ever seen." And of his death he said, "It hardly seemed credible that a life force like his, so generously endowed with the *rhythm* of motion through time, could be smothered and shut down at such an early age. ... Neal's death had hit me harder than I knew; I'd been obsessing on the loss of one of the most inspiring people I'd ever known personally. . . . I vowed to myself that in the future I would live up to Neal's inspirational example." [see, also, Phil Lesh chapter later in book]

McNally described him in his *Long Strange Trip* — "Disguised as a loony mad-rapping speed freak, Neal Cassady was very possibly the most highly evolved personality they would ever meet, and was certainly among their most profound life influences other than the psychedelic experience itself."

Even their first co-manager **Rock Scully** sketched the band's Beat birth in his memoir *Living with The Dead*: "The hungry i, Vesuvio's, and City Lights were our shrines. Kerouac, Kesey, Corso, Burroughs and Ginsberg were our holy madmen. We idolized the Beats ... Jerry was 15 when *On The Road* came out, and it became his bible ...."

The Dead's drummer **Bill Kreutzmann** described in his book *Deal* how he'd read *On The Road* before he'd met the rest of the band, and how "It became influential to me in the same way that certain music was influential. It was jazz, on the page. ... it was a boarding pass out of Palo Alto and into destinations unknown — my life's great adventure. ... that there was something greater out there, and even if it didn't appear within my reach, I could grab ahold of it anyway, just by believing it was possible. That's really important. Because after that, I started reaching for it. And sure enough, I was able to grab hold."

To *Garcia* biographer Blair Jackson, **Bob Weir** said, "When I fell in with Ken Kesey and Neal Cassady, it seemed like home sweet home to me, to be tossed in with a bunch of crazies. There was some real serious crazy stuff going on . . . For one thing I had to abandon all my previous conceptions of space and time. I thought I was pretty well indoctrinated into the 'anything goes' way of life, but I found much more than anything goes with the Pranksters. There was a world of limitless possibilities. It's hard to say anything that doesn't sound clichéd, but it was really a whole new reality for this boy. We were dealing with stuff like telepathy on a daily basis.

"We picked up a lot from those guys. Particularly

from Cassady. He was able to drive 50 miles-an-hour through downtown rush-hour traffic. He could see around corners — I don't know how to better describe it. And that's useful if you're playing improvisational music; you can build those skills to see around corners, 'cause there are plenty of corners that come up. We gleaned that kind of approach from Cassady. He was one of our teachers, as well as a playmate."

Another time Weir went even furthur — "We're all siblings, we're all underlings to this guy Neal Cassady. He had the guiding hand." Describing hanging with Neal, he said, "It was pretty free-form, but it was also — I hate to use the word cosmic, but I don't know how else to describe it. We were together in this big mind meld, and he would be having a conversation with what was going on inside your head." (Something innumerable people have also confessed.)

"His life is nowhere near over," Weir told *On The Road* director Walter Salles decades after Neal's passing. "He lives in me and through me, especially when I'm on stage. He was more present than any human I've ever met. What I didn't learn I just osmoted from him. Living purely and completely in The Moment. What he saw in the present was an accumulation of all things past and future. 'Now' is all he was really involved with. That's what I've always drawn from when I'm playing — forget everything and just *be there*."

And as Furthur proof — in a recent filmed interview with Weir at his new TRI Studios, in the background there is only one piece of artwork hanging in the whole place — a GIANT photograph of Neal Cassady.

Original Prankster and Cassady friend **Paul Foster** once described him — "Others can talk fast, but slowed down it's poppycock. Play Neal at 33 and it's interesting, voluminous, humorous, often rhyming and intimidatingly encyclopedic in that he was enormously well read and he could handle simultaneously eight channels of audio interchange, including items from all radios and televisions he had turned on, random street noise,

8

conversations within earshot and several secret thoughts, it would all enter the fabric, the nap of his rap."

As Prankster second-in-command, **Kapn Ken Babbs** put it to Beatdom magazine, "Kesey and I fell in the crack between the Beat and Psychedelic generations. Too young for one, too old for the other. Cassady was the link between the two. He introduced us to the Beats and was with us during the Psychedelic Revolution. We rode the psychedelic wave, were on the crest, along with thousands of others. The wave continues to roll on, probably all the way to Kansas by now. Our role is to keep the spirit alive. Freedom reigns on us all, savor it."

About the commonality between both the Beats and Pranksters traveling America on the open Road, he said, "The car had a tremendous impact on our lives. The word peon means pedestrian. The car was an enabler. It enabled us to travel in meatspace, the windshield our TV screen, a constantly changing panorama as we raced out of the past through the present and into the future. Signs

Carolyn Cassady and Ken Babbs at the 1982 On The Road
Conference in Boulder.

in bars said, Free Beer Tomorrow. It's time travel on the surface of the earth and you can stop and get out whenever you want. True liberation."

He also riffed on the Pranksters picking up the Beat torch: "The Beat goes on — expanding through psychedelic awakenings and awarenesses of spontaneous eruptions of joy and glee in order to puncture the balloons of stuffy rigid necked spouters of ancient ugly arguments."

Wavy Gravy confessed — "I was a teenage beatnik."
:-)

The national news story that was the *Howl* obscenity trial probably did more than any other single event to promote the Beats nationwide. And through that, there became an awareness and proliferation of poetry readings that people like Hugh Romney (pre "Wavy Gravy") jumped all over. Being both artist and organizer, he quickly put together a Beat reading underneath The Rock on Huntington Ave. in Boston, decorating it all in black, the official color for cool cats in the late '50s. He then used his muster pay from leaving the army to open a jazz-poetry club in Kennebunkport Maine called Cafe on The Square where he read his own poetry to live jazz.

By 1958 he relocated to New York City to become part of the legendary Neighborhood Playhouse that at the time had already been home to Gregory Peck, Steve McQueen, Eli Wallach, and prior to just about every actor you've ever heard of passing through its doors. But he was quickly drawn to the full-on Bohemia of Greenwich Village, and in no time had parlayed himself into being the booker at The Gaslight Cafe on MacDougal Street which was the epicenter of the downtown Beat poetry scene. This was the place where the Beat (and then 'nik) concept started of snapping your fingers in approval rather than clapping because there were air shafts that went from the basement club to the upstairs apartments and the frequent applause would disturb the tenants.

While running the shows there, he suggested to the owner, legendary Village raconteur John Mitchell, that he should have folk singers in among the poets, which led directly to another young artist who was heavily influenced by the Beats and *On The Road*, Bob Dylan, to start doing some of his first acoustic shows in New York in that subterranean cellar. That same year, 1961, Wavy was the opening performer at a new club on Bleecker Street called The Bitter End that's still there to this day, and where that same young folk singer would later put together his Rolling Thunder tour in the mid-'70s.

"But the connecting rod between the Beats and the Pranksters was Neal Cassady," Wavy told me recently. "He drove Kerouac's car and Kesey's bus. That was the guy. It was such a thrill to ride shotgun with him, cuz Neal would be rolling a J and pealing an orange and carrying on three different conversations while making a fast left turn and double clutching all at the same time.

"Some of the greatest moments of my life were spent sharing the microphone with Neal Cassady. I remember one night something funny happened in the audience while we were up there, and Cassady was zooming along and didn't stop. And I said, 'Hold on — Time-out. You have to laugh when something funny happens or I don't want to play anymore.' And Neal suddenly realized the moment, and actually blushed, which is something I don't think happened very often.

"Neal was always doing ten things at once and nothing twice. I knew Allen and Kerouac and a bunch of them from the Gaslight days — I once drank a gallon of Gallo with Jack on the Lower East Side one night — but Cassady was my real connection to that scene. I loved that guy."

Kesey talked about first meeting Cassady as a Stanford student in that *Paris Review* interview — "He was running around, this frenetic, crazed character speaking in a monologue that sounded like *Finnegans Wake* played fast forward. . . . I realized then that there was a choice. Cassady had gone down one road. I thought to myself — Are you going to go down that road with Burroughs, Ginsberg, and Kerouac — at that time still unproven crazies — or are you going to take the safer road that leads to John Updike. Cassady was a hero to all of us who followed the wild road, the hero who moved us all."

When asked in the same interview about what he learned from Cassady, he said, "I've tried to distill his teachings as best I can. ... His most powerful lesson behind the rap was to not dwell on mistakes. He used the metaphor of driving. He believed you get into trouble by overcorrecting. ... Cassady believed you had to be correcting every instant. The longer you let things go, the longer you stayed comfortable, the more likely the case that you would have to overcorrect. Then you would have created a big error. The virtue of continual, engaged existence — an endless and relentless argument with the self — that was his lesson."

Somebody who was there the moment the idea for The Bus first sparked, **George Walker,** aka **Hardly Visible,** became it's chief mechanic and main driver besides Neal. As Robert Hunter said, it was hard to *not* be Neal after he was around, and George spent more time with Cassady than pretty much anybody else in the last several years of his life, and to this day brings Neal to life on a stage at shows all over the continent (with yours unruly in the role of Jack), [see: BrianHassett.com for details] and still naturally raps in fast-paced riffs about any subject you put in front of him.

"We were about a shift in consciousness, and advancing our souls. Traditional religions weren't filling the bill, and we wanted something deeper. We were trying to go beyond the restraints of American society. It wasn't just about having fun, we were all on our own journeys, and we wanted to be part of making a difference. That was really what the Pranksters were about. And *On The Road* was one of the pieces that first gave us a glimpse of the map of where we might go. Kerouac drew the map, but it was Cassady who took us on the road and guided us through it."

Kesey biographer Robert Faggen wrote in his "The Beats and The 1960s" essay in *The Cambridge History of the American Novel*: "Any notion that the Beats were merely about being 'rebels' or 'cool' or 'counterculture' ignores the fundamental positive aim apparent in almost all their writing — a desire for some kind of liberation toward a better and spiritual plane of existence. However much that vision became denigrated, parodied, or sold out, it was a fundamental part of the writing from the beginning — even in the very conception of Beat."

Of Cassady taking the wheel, Walker said, "That was really when everything changed — when Neal announced he was going to drive The Bus. He showed up with all his tire changing tools — which was a good thing because all the tires were about ready to go. He ended up putting on every tire that's on The Bus, and they're still there holding the air Neal put into them.

"Without Kerouac there would have been no Pranksters," he let me know without equivocation. "And with Cassady we became something more than we ever could have without. Ginsberg was around quite a bit, too, and he was a real spiritual guy, but it was Neal who drove us in more ways than one.

"I was there the night we all got together in the apartment in **New York in '64, the last time Jack and Neal ever saw each other.** It was the only time I ever met Jack. He was real quiet, and we were real loud, as we always were. We were all having a big party, and he wasn't into what we were doing. If you see the footage or the photos from the party, you don't see many shots of Ken and Jack together, or even Jack and Neal.

"Neal was very perceptive, and he probably realized this wasn't going as he hoped, and kind of retreated. Kesey really dominated the scene, as he almost always did, and Jack was just listening and watching and pounding Budweisers. At one point Kesey put a flag around Kerouac's neck, but there was a reluctance. He didn't want to get involved. He seemed real uncomfortable, is the way I remember it."

The party was held at 1239 Madison Avenue between 89th & 90th Streets where Kesey's Perry Lane friend Chloe Scott was house-sitting her aunt's apartment. "I think it was ten or eleven at night when Neal brought Jack to the apartment," **Ginsberg recalled** in the book *On The Bus.* "Neal and Jack stayed down in the bus with Peter Orlovsky and myself for a while, then we went upstairs. The Pranksters had a big throne of a sofa completely clear for Kerouac. The room was full of wires and lights and cameras and people in striped clothes and Pranksters and jesters and American flags and people waving cameras around drinking in rock and roll and lit up like amphetamines.

"Kerouac didn't say much and was quite ill. He was also ill at ease, not because of Kesey but because of his physical condition. But Kesey was smart enough to recognize Kerouac and respect him for what he was doing. He saw him as sort of an elder master and a great American. ... Neal did put himself out trying to accommodate Kerouac, but, in a way, that was nerve-wracking because he had roused Kerouac without any notice, and driven him back to the city to a big party full of people who were taking amphetamines and acid and running around with cameras and klieg lights."

Kesey's Stanford writing pal **Robert Stone** also came to the party and reflected back on it in the same book, "Kerouac was a guy who was basically very sweet who soured over the years. I think alcohol and the ridicule from the press were really getting to him. ... Instead of treating Kerouac as a serious author, he was treated as a joke. He encouraged it in a way because he was always showing up drunk and clowning, but the columnists, the newspapers, and the magazines really did treat Kerouac like a joke. ... In those days there was this nasty hostility toward nonconformists, and Kerouac endured a lot of it."

Kerouac and Kesey's literary agent, **Sterling Lord** (yes — the same guy represented both!), wrote of the get-together of two of his legendary clients in his memoir, *Lord of Publishing.* "Ken and several other Pranksters were eager to meet Jack because they had been deeply influenced by *On the Road.* I told Kerouac that Kesey was going to be in town and would be in touch with him. Cassady contacted Allen Ginsberg, and the two of them,

14

along with Peter Orlovsky, Allen's partner, and Peter's brother Julius, who was one day out of a 14-year stay in a mental institution, drove out to Northport on Long Island to pick up Kerouac and bring him into Manhattan.

"Jack was 12 years older than Ken, and there was a marked difference in their energies and interests. Jack had been living in a house with his mother in Northport, although he still had to deal from time to time with the public adulation inspired by the 1957 publication of *On the Road*. His was a relatively passive life. Kesey and the Pranksters, on the other hand, were on an extended high that peaked in New York."

Babbs recalled it pretty much the same way to Beatdom: "Jack was tired. He'd been through a lot by 1964. Any time someone is said to be the spokesman for something, it takes a lot out of you, either denying it or trying to rise to it. I'm sure Jack had seen plenty of shenanigans the likes of the Merry Pranksters, so our cavorting was nothing new to him. He was kind and gracious, very patient, but after a while he left the apartment where Cassady and Ginsberg and Peter Orlovsky had brought him to meet us. I definitely, after it was all over, had the sense the torch was being passed."

In that same *Paris Review* interview with Bob Faggen, Kesey remembered it: "I have thought about that meeting hundreds of times since then. We wanted Kerouac to be the same way he was when he wrote *On The Road*. I find the same thing happening to me when people show up and expect me to be the way I was 25 years ago. Kerouac seemed offended by our wildness . . . I was disappointed in myself for not going up to him and sincerely expressing how much his work meant to me."

After Jack died, Ken wrote his widow Stella. "I told her that I couldn't hold a candle to him. His life's work will stand for centuries. I believe people will be reading *On The Road* centuries from now as the true lens into our time. In his writing Kerouac was true to his vision to the end. He believed there were drama and glory in the most mundane parts of our lives. And all things —

running across a football field, the smell of leafs, the sound of a car — became charged with romance in Kerouac's imagination. He was part of the ongoing exploration of the American frontier, looking for new land, trying to escape the dust bowls of existence. He had a deep connection to the American romantic vision. Kerouac was a giant to the end, a sad giant. But then giants are usually sad."

George Walker continued riffing, "Kerouac was a great help in us finding our cool. We were always looking for a kool place, like the movie title says, and he seemed to have what we were all looking for in those early days. He was a leader in the direction we wanted to go. But Cassady was our real connection to it all. I really got to know and understand him. It started with our mutual love of jazz. That was our first bond. And cars were our second.

"He really believed in reincarnation and karma. He was all about advancing our consciousness, our spirits, our soul ... but he was really conflicted. I'm writing a book about his last days and death, and he talked a lot about 'cleaning up' ... both his soul and his life ... it was what he was striving for but he just couldn't get there. Neal was like a child in his enthusiasm, like the way a little kid might gush, "Dad! Dad! I gotta show you something!!" not worrying about whether it's acceptable or appropriate, just unabashed blind enthusiasm. That's what Neal was like."

Merry Prankster cousin and close Kesey friend since they edited *The Last Supplement of The Whole Earth Catalog* together, lifelong funny-guy **Paul Krassner**, told Beatdom about the Beat Generation — "It was reassuring to see it as a counterculture movement even before the word was invented. I identified with their spirit of irreverence toward authority. And I liked the individuals I met, such as Allen Ginsberg and Gregory Corso, whose lives were as poetic as their writing. I think there's always been a counterculture, from the Bohemians to the Beats to the Hippies to the Yippies to the Punks to Hip-Hop. It probably started during cave-dwelling days; while the adults were drawing on the walls of their caves, the kids were out in the field making their marks on boulders."

16

Talking about the role of humor in the whole
endeavor, he said, "Humor seems to be part of an innate
tradition. It can be a means of revealing the truth and
waking up people while having fun in the process. For
me, viewing reality through the prism of absurdity has
become a way of life. Humor can relieve tension, unite
people from disparate backgrounds, and medical research
has shown that laughter can serve as an aid to healing,
physically & psychologically."

Original Prankster **Linda Breen**, named
Anonymous because she jumped on The Bus in Calgary
in '64 as a 15-year-old runaway and had to remain
undercover, told me, "I read *On The Road* when I was 13.
It was risque then, but I just *felt* that way. It was the first
thing that connected with me, really. Jack's way of just
going out in the world and doing things. It became my
bible. And it's still a part of me to this day, like my bones.
It's the hard structure the rest of me is built around.

"Growing up in Canada, my parents gave me the
freedom to explore things on my own. It's why I was so
free, in my mind, to just Get On The Bus. When I first
saw it there at the Stampede, I was just, 'Oh my goodness!
Look at that!!' It was Gretchen Fetchin that I first saw.
She was so happy. And they were dancing in a circle
around the Bus. There were maybe a hundred people
standing there watching them, jaw-dropped. And I just
went right up and asked Hagen if I could ride with them,
and that was it.

"Then when we got to California I met Neal. Ken
sidled up to me and told me, 'You know you're living in a
book, right?' I had no idea. But it all made sense. He had
a super big impact on my life. I remember him driving
The Bus and sitting beside him on an apple crate and
watching him take on life, embrace everything that came at
him without fear, and all with this multi-layered narration
and storytelling.

"When he drove, his wings were flapping and he just
flew! It was like he was dancing on the gears and pedals.
And he took me under his wing and I danced with him. He

17

was very kind, and embraced me in an emotional way, and really helped me on my journey. I'm getting emotional just thinking about him," as her voice indeed was cracking. "I'm glad I was able to tell his daughter Jami this recently. I'm so glad there's been such a resurgence of interest in him and all this stuff.

"To me the message of *On The Road* and the Pranksters was to be alive. Feel free. Being with them, every day felt like the first day of summer when you were a kid. 'No more pencils, no more books, no more teacher's dirty looks.' We were all young and happy and we danced. I was finally living the life I knew had to be out there somewhere. Jack first told me so — and then Ken and Neal made it a reality."

Roy Sebern, the artist and original Prankster who first painted "FURTHUR" on the front of The Bus (playing with the 'you are'), explained to me recently how they were living in a Beat Bohemia at Perry Lane (which was actually, technically, an Avenue, but they all called it "Perry Lane" or just "The Lane") near Stanford University in Palo Alto, which he moved into in 1959: "We were all unique individuals pursuing different arts and disciplines, but there was a Beat overlay.

"I first read *On The Road* in 1958. I was raised Methodist, and read *The Bible* and was used to reading books to find answers and learn. I was on a spiritual quest and looking for the meaning of life and questioning the realities of life as they were presented. When I read *On The Road* it seemed like a flashing blueprint of what to do next — go on the road! And that's what I did — hitchhiking to New York because of Kerouac's tales. It seemed like this mythical place where the energy of the world was concentrated. I had set out on a vision quest that I'm still on."

Journalist and Adventurer **Lee Quarnstrom**, one of those famously arrested with Kesey at the La Honda raid in 1965, told me of his journey that began with Jack: "When I read about Zen after reading Kerouac — first *The Town and the City* then *On The Road* — was the concept

18

There wasn't a bridge between the Beats and the Pranksters — it was just a loving embrace. Levi Asher, Merry Prankster Anonymous with Big Al Hinkle & Tom Lake — at the Beat Museum in S.F., June 2015

of Darshan, accumulating grace by being in the presence of others, 'high' people, bodhisattvas, I guess -- who had grace to give. I never thought about it at the time, but I was gathering (without actively knowing it) grace from such bodhisattvas as Kesey and Neal Cassady and Allen Ginsberg and a handful of other men & women I've shared my life with. Pranksters used to refer to that grace, that cosmic force, as 'Cosmo.' I've thought I might retitle my book as *Shaking Hands with Cosmo*, only that sounds a little pretentious, don't you think? I guess I'll keep *When I Was a Dynamiter, or How a Nice Catholic Boy Became a Merry Prankster, a Pornographer and a Bridegroom Seven Times*. I like it. Maybe I'll write another book so I can use the title!"

Denise Kaufman — also known by her Kesey-bestowed Prankster name "Mary Microgram" — told me, "I came along just after the Beats. I was sneaking off and taking the bus to North Beach in the early '60s when I was 14, 15, 16, going to City Lights and the coffeeshops.

As Ken pointed out to me, I was lucky to have come of age in a world that they'd sparked changes in. I'd read Ferlinghetti's *Coney Island of The Mind* and Allen Ginsberg and all that, but it was advanced consciousness I was interested in — whether that was through drugs or yoga or meditation or music or Tibetan Buddhism.

"I used to ride shotgun a lot on a metal box next to Neal on Kesey's Bus," she went on. "That was my place. If you closed your eyes and listened to him while he was driving it was like your brain was being rearranged. He wasn't a leader like Kesey and Babbs were. He was just a phenomenon, flowing through the whole scene. He might have been older in years, but he wasn't *anyone's* concept of 'old.' He was so full of energy and life and exuberance. And the acuity of his memories astounded me."

As the literary agent Sterling Lord reflected back on his two clients, "Kesey was not a part of the Beat Generation. Thanks to a CIA-funded drug experiment at a veterans hospital, which had introduced Kesey to psychedelic drugs, Kesey instead sparked the Psychedelic Revolution, which spawned the hippie movement. Kesey brought LSD to people's awareness, and he and the Merry Pranksters spoke of its mind-expanding, life-enhancing properties.

"Kerouac was of course not a part of that revolution. What I realized was that Jack was deeply committed to writing. Kesey was just as deeply committed to living and experiencing the lives of others; writing for him was just a part of living.

"The Beats and the Pranksters showed us different ways of opting out of society. They were both countercultural movements. The Beats were trying to change literature, and the Pranksters were trying to change the people and the country. After *Sometimes a Great Notion* was published in 1964 and Kesey moved into the next chapters of his life, he often said, when anyone asked him what he was doing, 'Our job is nothing less than saving the world.' And, 'The only true currency is that of the spirit.'

"Kerouac was basically shy when outside his own milieu and in no way a self-promoter. But he lived much of the time in New York or nearby Long Island, and at least during the '50s was accessible to the media, although he did not seek publicity or present himself well in public. They came to him. *On the Road* had electrified the literary community and sharply marked the arrival of a new

Ken Kesey and the author at the Jack Kerouac On The Road Conference in Boulder, 1982

generation, and he made good copy for the newspapers.

"Kesey was anything but shy. He embraced people; he gave of himself to others. *One Flew Over the Cuckoo's Nest* was the debut of a daring new voice, but in the end, Kesey's profound impact on his generation and those to come was the result of his whole style of life — novels, bus trips, acid tests, public performances, and the like. Also, Kesey didn't seek out the press and he lived so far away from what earlier journalists called the ballyhoo belt — New York City. Besides, as he put it, fame gets in the way of creativity."

One other connection I have no proof of — but that doesn't mean it isn't true — is that the central character in the central book of Kesey's canon is the same central character in the central book of Kerouac's canon. The Chief tells us Randle's story, and Sal tells us Dean's.

Knowing of Kesey's association with Cassady, I assumed for years that **Randle Patrick McMurphy** in *Cuckoo's Nest* was based on Cassady — until I found out it was written and published before Neal ever showed up in Ken's driveway at 9 Perry Lane in 1962 — the reason for his unexpected arrival never disclosed to Kesey or anyone else — until George Walker recently got to the bottom of it:

"When Neal showed up, Kesey had just returned from working on *Sometimes a Great Notion* in Oregon. The first indication of his arrival were sounds of a commotion outside, and there was an old Jeep station wagon in the driveway, the back end jacked up off the ground, with somebody under it, feet protruding. That somebody turned out to be Cassady, attempting to fix some mechanical problem, and muttering to nobody in particular about the problem.

"Suddenly aware of other's presence, Neal crawled out from under the Jeep and introduced himself to Ken and his friends Roy Sebern, Jane Burton, Jim Wolpman, and maybe Vic Lovell and a few others, all of whom were immediately taken with Neal's verbosity and frenetic manner, and didn't know what to make of it until they realized this man was the model for Dean Moriarty.

"People think Neal came to meet Kesey after reading *Cuckoo's Nest*, but that was not the case. In fact, Neal had neither read the book (yet), nor even heard of it, and he wasn't there to meet Kesey at all. He had come to see his friend Rom Bondoc, who was living there at #9 with his wife Gigi during Ken's absence.

"Rom was in his third year at Stanford Law School, and was somewhat ahead of the time in that he had been a pot smoker for years before most of his friends discovered it. Cassady, of course, had been smoking "tea" with Kerouac and Ginsberg

& company for years, and this was a reason for the friendship between he and Rom.

"In short, Neal came to Perry Lane to get high with Rom Bondoc, and was surprised to find Kesey living in the house where his friend had been staying.

"With his ingratiating if somewhat strange demeanor, it wasn't long before Neal was accepted into the Perry Lane community, and soon became a regular visitor. When The Lane was demolished a year or so later, the Keseys moved to their forest home in La Honda, where Cassady continued to come by somewhat regularly.

"Oh, yes, despite his well-earned reputation as a less than expert mechanic, Neal somehow managed to diagnose and fix the problem with the Jeep. This we know, as it was driven away later that day. The Jeep was gone, but Neal's spirit was there to stay."

McMurphy was a charismatic good-looking fast-talking Irish jailbird conman and master manipulator who had a way with women. He instigated road trips, and stole a boat for a joyride in place of a car. He had the gift of gab and unflinching confidence. He loved to play and goof and get away with whatever he could between the cracks. He sure seemed like Dean Moriarty in *On The Road* to me. "McMurphy" & "Moriarty" even sound alike. And not fer nuthing but Jack Nicholson coulda played the hell outta both of them with manic aplomb. :-)

Kesey told Faggen in the *Paris Review* interview, "The Irish names — Kesey, Cassady, McMurphy — were all together in my mind as well as a sense of Irish blarney. That's part of the romantic naiveté of McMurphy. But McMurphy was born a long time before I met Neal Cassady. The character of McMurphy comes from Sunday matinees, from American Westerns. He's Shane that rides into town, shoots the bad guys, and gets killed in the course of the movie."

And indeed, both *Cuckoo's Nest* and *Road* end on sad notes for their heroes. Or *antiheroes*. Yet their lives as recounted lifted them to legend.

And legend and myth are a big part of it. "It's true even if it didn't happen," Kesey would say with his leprechaun twinkle. Or there's his oft-quoted, "To hell with facts. We need stories!" Kerouac called his collected work "The Duluoz Legend" — unabashedly mythologizing and fictionalizing his real life. Playing with reality is both an author's and a Prankster's mission. As is having fun and Adventure — *and capturing it.* As is "tootling the multitudes" and practicing "first thought best thought."

Kerouac wrote on an endless scroll. Kesey filmed an endless movie. Both were shaking up the conventions of America, which by 1964 was still not much different than 1954. The Beats were the blooming and the Pranksters the fruition. The Beats were the sprouts from the garden earth and the Pranksters the flowers that turned black & white to color and became something you could wear in your hair and turn round from square.

Kerouac captured the discovery of America by post-WWII modes and means . . . and the Pranksters turned it into a Bus with beans. Kerouac made literature fun ... and the Pranksters made living funny. Kerouac opened up possibilities and the Pranksters closed the deal.

On The Road was the cardkey pocketbook you needed to pull out of your back pocket to get through the door of The Bus. Neal Cassady was the guy who drove Kerouac on the most important Road trip of his life, then did the same for Kesey — in case anyone missed the obvious. Kerouac lived through and captured the birth of BeBop, and Kesey created the Acid Tests that birthed The Grateful Dead and the psychedelic revolution. Kerouac and Kesey are next to each other in most alphabetical lists of great 20th century authors — but they were also 1, 2 in a much bigger chronology. And so much of the world is still On The Road and On The Bus.

2

Lowell Celebrates Kerouac 2016

In the Spirit of Jack — a spontaneous love ode that just flowed ...
To that thing they do in Lowell . . .

What's cool about LCK is — everybody's there for Jack . .
. but all on their own terms.
Everybody has a completely different relationship with their family member.
You'll hear a hundred different stories
all by people beaming in front of you
radiating energy;
coming from England or Germany or France or Canada
or Indiana or Kansas or Florida or Texas,
because of *On The Road* or *Maggie Cassidy* or *Dr. Sax*
because of America or Walt Whitman or Dr. Thompson
because of wanderlust or adventure or a Doctoral thesis.

There's all the guided firsthand tours you wanna ride,
and historians and scholars next to you wherever you
roam,
and playful people off the clock just riffin in the beauty
of all the assembled happiness.

There's nonstop jamming and goofing and hugging
interaction.
And there's a million places to go — both on maps and
not —
Dr. Sax's woods
the Merrimack's banks
the cobblestone streets and brick building labyrinths.

And all the local Lowell Jacksters come out from all
their local hidings —
for the weekend they can let their freak flag fly.
And everybody's got stories.
And you hear Jack lines you've read play back in your
head,
as you walk with a krewe of your new best friends
from one scene to another
in places you've only imagined
and some you haven't even!

And it goes on for days ... and days ...
From the setting sunlit Worthen afternoon of Thursday
—
leading into the epic "bar crawl" of Jack's joints that
climaxes at Cappy's Copper Kettle (of Fish) with David
Amram riffin' *Pull My Daisy* ...
Until homeboy Bill Walsh's final walking tour on
Monday thru the secret lairs of Pawtucketville
which weaves back into our Worthen clubhouse
where the worthy who made it all the way
hoist and toast until the jam is done.

It's Jack in the now.
Not in books.
Not online.
In person.
In front of you.
Right now.

Live it
or
lose it.

More Beats and Pranksters!
The Wizard of Wonder makes Jack's principle musical
collaborator David Amram an honorary Merry
Prankster with the bestowing of the official wristband at
Lowell Celebrates Kerouac.
But as Wiz lovingly observed, "David was a Prankster
long before Kesey & Babbs ever came up with it!"

3

Shindig Sutra

Aahhh — San Francisco — home of everything holy.
   Home of the Beats, home of The Dead, home
of the wild. The United States of San Francisco. The
city that makes its own rules . . . and that's that.
   Of *course* we're coming home. To the
Museum that Jerry built. Cimino, that is. The Beat
Museum. Of *course* there *has* to be a Beat Museum.
How could there not be?
   Just like that other Jerry from San Francisco
started another institution that never died — Jerry
2.0 has finally put brick-&-mortar to an idea that was
always in the air there.
   And just as The Museum was his lifelong dream
— so too was having a summit a la Boulder '82 that
he almost went to but missed by a hair.
   And like a fat book that reads really fast, the
million events and people in this weekend orgy of
words and ideas passed in the blink of some beautiful
eyes.
   First there was the *pre*–opening party. I mean,
it's all about the parties, let's face it. And a company
that accents beautiful eyes — Warby Parker — the
high-end glasses shop named for a couple different
character names the Jack-loving owner's noticed in

29

Kerouac's notebooks at the NYPL show — decided
to throw us a Welcome-to-Town Party complete with
jazz trio and poetry readings and a typewriter to riff
your own spontaneous bop prosody.

But things *really* kicked into gear Friday night
with the official Opening Night Party that took over
the entire two floors of this action-packed Museum,
with all the wine and craft beer you could drink. Tom
Waits, the Dead and '50s jazz played from the
speakers in every ceiling corner. And filling every
floor corner were Beats new and old.

There's **ruth weiss**! Finally! Never met her
before — with her blazing blue-green-tourquoise hair
— an idea she got from a movie called *"The Boy
With The Green Hair"* that she saw as a 20-year-old
— and was still dancing on the balls of her feet and
bopping with more energy than the 20-somethings.

There was **Gerd (pronounced Gaird) Stern** —
the man who did NOT lose The Joan Anderson Letter
— who I was hosting his talk tomorrow and had
just met a couple days earlier on this secret sacred
houseboat The Vallejo which he lived on at one time
and was still in the same harbor he called home in
the '40s & '50s. And there's him and ruth seeing each
other for the first time in 50 years!

And there's Big **Al Hinkle**! Who's not quite as

with Al Hinkle and Jami Cassady

towering as he once was but is still a giant of a man at 88. He was of course a star attraction — "The Last Man Standing" — the only guy who was in the car On The Road who's still here to tell about it. And tell about it he does with a great memory and all his faculties and senses with him. And there's **Jami "Jack's favorite" Cassady** and husband Randy who are keeping the family torch burning bright after losing the matriarch just a couple years ago. Jami's the most friendly, easy-to-smile, Spirit-filled being you could ever hope to meet. Growing up with Neal & Carolyn and Uncle Jack and Uncle Allen she's seen it all and then some — so she always remains beatifically tranquil in any kind of maelstrom of madness.

And Next-Gen Merry Prankster Moray brought the original **Anonymous** who got On The Bus in Calgary as a 15 year old after having just read *On The Road* and, as she says, she was *born* "on the bus" — and was as tickled to be hanging with the Beat Founders as any of us.

And there's **Levi Asher** — my old brother of the Greenwich Village Beat scene shows of the '90s and 2000s — who I helped produce the big celebration for his web-pioneering LitKicks — their 5th anniversary at The Bitter End in 1999 with a symmetrical 9 hours of non-stop show . . . from a drumming sage-burning opening to John Cassady leading an all-star jam until 4AM.

And this weekend was the same damn thing — non-stop from Friday til . . . Tuesday, to be perfectly honest.

And there's long-time Beat **Neeli Cherkovski** in the role of Gregory Corso — the portly disheveled poet always surrounded by a coterie of confederates on some mischievous mission of madness. And there's **Chris Felver** workin' the room — the unofficial official Beat photographer and one of the five who were here in 2015 and there in '82.

And there's **Dan Barth** another of the Boulder '82ers who read there at Allen's Oracles on the closing Sunday night and became the Poet Laureate of Mendocino County and travelled down from The Great Green North to spread his Zen Beat poetry in the city lights.

And if you're wondering — **David Amram** and **Dennis McNally** were the other two Boulder '82ers — but they wouldn't appear until tomorrow.

And there's **Hilary Holladay** who founded the Kerouac Studies program at U. Mass. in Lowell, and just wrote the Huncke book, and brought out a bunch of her students from Virginia who were smart, polite and Beat to their core.

And there's **Tom Galasso** who lived with Edie Kerouac in Detroit and is one of the few around I can swap first-hand stories with of Jack's first long-term love.

And then **Tom Lake** appears — the major Beat player online ... known the guy for years ... never met 'im ... until I hear somebody say, "I'm Tom Lake," and I turn around ... and it's the blind guy with the white cane!

Wait — what? The guy I've been interacting with online for years ... is *blind*?!

No.

But yes! And we bond like brothers and he ends up being a playful prankster sidekick for this entire Shindigian Adventure!

Which also included of course hangin' at the Hudson . . .

and getting *him* to take photographs . . . (!)

a blind guy's photography . . .

making art that he can't experience

except by hearing other people's reactions to it.

And there's my **Wight brother** Orville, another longtime onliner I'm meeting for the first time and who's been On The Road forever, dancing on both sides of the Jerry–Jack fuzzy line ...

And there's the beaming **Shelly Musgrove** who I first met over photos from Vesuvio's and has been on a crash course in Beatlandia, including devouring my book in one sitting, and traveling halfway across the state to be here.

And this whole packed-Museum opening-

night cocktail-party is running effortlessly
because of beatnik-clad show producers **Otto &
Baby Doe,** who've been doing off-Beat events
for decades, and have rounded up an army of
volunteers and liquifying sponsors, and weaving it
all seamlessly in with the Museum's inner cabinet
of **Brandon** the visual design guy, and **Bob** the
poetry organizer, and **E.T.** the novelist from another
planet, and **Niko** the sharp-dressed man disguising
the nature-loving poet revolutionary that all these
Museumistas seem to be.

And all the first-time meetings and long-time
reunions by so many segued naturally into a late
night hang at Vesuvio's across the street in a dance
of interactive eye-blazing joy and story sharing
across the universe.

Saturday — the first full day — was huge: **Dr. Philip
Hicks**, the psychiatrist who Allen credits with giving
him permission to be himself, spoke in public about
that landmark diagnosis for the first time. Current
San Francisco Poet Laureate **Alejandro Murguia**
riffed his imagistic word magic as a harmonizing
echo of Kerouac's paeans to The Mission's
downtrodden. The brilliant funny modern-day Lenny
Bruce / Mort Sahl of contemporary North Beach
— **Will Durst** — laid down his political and cultural
stand-up routine.

When I told him about the hitchhiking adventure of the book, he looked me deadpan in the eye and advised me — "You're crazy, you know that?"

Director **Heather Dalton** screened her new "*Neal Cassady – The Denver Years*" film in its West Coast premiere. Local Beat authority **Jonah Raskin** brought the history of the city to life in a multimedia show. The perpetually beaming **Tate Swindell** and his brother **Todd** made sure Jack Micheline and Harold Norse made it to the Shindig through film clips and audio recordings and first-hand stories. Neeli held a poetry workshop. Felver riffed on Ferlinghetti. And Amram performed his patented Jack music & storytelling revue.

And sitting outside in the secluded Fort Mason enclave that we took over along the northern shore of the city with Alcatraz in the distance were a bunch of late-'40s Hudsons bringing the material machines into the mindful mindfields of poetry and prose.

Inside the main building was this giant party room with a poetry & jazz stage; and all sorts of bookstores with tables of cool stuff; as well as the Cassadys set-up with Carolyn's easel and paintings and stuff; and there was a bar selling perfectly cold beer and wine. Across the outdoor atrium was an excellent cafe / restaurant with all sorts of healthy California delights to stay or go. What I'm sayin is — we were set! Self-contained. You could take a hundred trips without leaving the farm.

I hosted the Gerd Stern talk — of Joan Anderson letter fame — *The Holy Grail by The Holy Goof* — the letter that blew open the doors for Kerouac's writing and did NOT blow off a houseboat in Sausalito — like Ginzy pinned on Gerd sixty years ago when in fact Allen had submitted it someplace and just forgot!

As I say, I first met him a few days earlier on this famous giant historic houseboat called **the Vallejo** that was home to Alan Watts and all sorts of interesting people over the decades and where I had to sign a non-disclosure release just to step on board that said I wouldn't tell anyone where it is or even

34

take any cell phone pictures that might reveal its location by GPS.

We got along like two buds in a joint right from the git-go — jammin out the crazy storyline of his crazy life, so when we hit the stage that afternoon we were already makin' beautiful jokes together. We went through the whole sequence of what happened, when and where, from his first meeting Allen and Carl Solomon at the Psychiatric Institute in New Jersey in 1947, and how he gave the manuscripts back to Allen in '53, and his thoughts on why the story came into existence, and the whole yak was videotaped and is now on YouTube. It was a packed room — and Jami Cassady was in the back beaming through the whole thing, and Levi Asher was in the front nodding in grooving agreement the whole time, and by all accounts it was a joyous jam.

As soon as this was over I had to bolt upstairs to the main theater to be part of the Cassady Family Panel with Al Hinkle and Jami Cassady, who asked me to be on it cuz I was pretty close to Carolyn n all. Brother John was supposed to be there, and we kept thinking he'd suddenly come bursting through the curtain and onto the stage but it never happened.

Good ol' Levi Asher was hosting, which I thought was great since we'd known each other for 20 years — until I realized — Al's known Jami since her birth day! He's seen her grow from a baby to a child to a mother to a grandmother . . . so he really knew the whole arc of the Cassady clan . . . and was the first person you ever heard of who met Neal!

And get this — **he & Neal were actually a circus act for a while!**

When they were both around 13, they were going to the same YMCA in Denver. Both of them were uncommonly strong for their age, and "that Y had the only high-wire circus act program in the country," Al said. "The big net, the trapeze, the whole schmear. And I found out later it had been donated by the great uncle of Hal Chase. (!)

"I thought it would be fun. The first thing you had to do was climb up and jump and land in the net — on your back if possible, so you'd bounce right up. And then they taught you how to roll over and use your hands and get off onto your feet. Then they had us swinging on the trapeze and dropping to the net.

"They said to me — because I was almost six feet tall then, and I was thin and had a little muscle — they said why don't you hang from the trapeze by your knees and see if you can catch somebody. They have a rope to the trapeze, and they pull it back, and get you going, and then they have another trapeze going the other way, and they'd have a guy there, and the only one that could do it was Neal.

"And then they wanted him to somehow do a flip, a roll, and then I'd catch him . . . and it seemed like that was pretty easy to do! We'd catch each other's wrists. He'd catch my wrists and I'd catch his — and it seemed like ... *we could do it!* And we practiced and practiced and got so we could do it most every time. And they had some other acts — I don't remember — they had a tumbling act, and a human pyramid, I remember that because I was on the bottom of the pyramid.

"So . . . we put on two shows. And people's parents were there. And we had a dress rehearsal type thing. I was supposed to catch Neal twice in each show. And I did on the first one — I caught him both times — and I missed him once at the second show. I think he came out of the summersault wrong or something, and he just went down — Boom! But he landed good.

"And then when summer was over, he was going to one school and I was going to another. I didn't even know his last name. We lost track of each other, and I never saw him again until we were both about 19 years old, and Jimmy Holmes, who was an old high school friend, he introduced us at Pederson's Pool Hall.

"I was just back from the Merchant Marines, and one day I'm walking down the street and bumped into Jimmy. I had a 1936 LaSalle convertible with a straight-8, and Jimmy had me come pick him up one Saturday, and I parked about a block away from the pool hall. And of course Jimmy knew everybody there, and we played a game of pool, and he was practically running the tables, just kinda showin' off, and we're just hanging out there, and then who comes in the back door, but Neal! And I looked at him, and he looked at me, and it didn't register at first. And I kept thinking about it, and I guess he was thinking about it, too. And then we finally made the connection.

"Then at some point I made the mistake of saying I have to go move my car, and right away he went, 'You've got a car?!?!'" and Al laughs heartily at the memory. "Now I'm his best friend!"

"He says, 'Would you mind if we took a drive to the drive-in? My wife works there.' On the ride over we reminisced about the circus together. Anyway, we get there and LuAnne's working as a car-hop. And I'm thinking, 'Boy she is *a beautiful girl!'*. .. but really young. I guess she was 16 at the time .... and they were married. And we have a Coke or something, and then we go back to the poolhall, and Neal and Jimmy start playing pool, and then these two girls come in the back door, and Neal goes over and gives one of them a big kiss, and introduces me

to his girlfriend!!

"Those were the first two times Neal and I hung out together."

And all sorts of stuff like this is going down. And once again the whole thing is on the Brian Hassett channel on YouTube.

But then the deal was — see, John Cassady was supposed to be on the panel — then we were gonna drive-like-Neal from there to the Dead show in Santa Clara — basically back to San Jose where he lives. . . . But the guy never showed!

And I dunno how this happens — just the magic of the universe — but I'm in the post-show hang with people in front of the stage and mention to somebody I gotta get from Levi's panel to Levi's Stadium . . . in a hurry. And this girl overhears me and says, "I wanna go there, too. You don't have an extra ticket, do you?" Well, as a matter of absent-John-fact, I think I do. "Well I've got a car." BOOM! Dun and Duner. And Weir outta there in a Flash!

Just like Boulder '82 — The Grateful Dead are playing smack in the middle of this Big Beat Conference. Who are these guys, and why do they keep following me around?

So we have this whole massive insane Adventure . . . the Dead's opening night of their 50th anniversary Farewell to home-base California — prophet on the golden shore and all that — but it'll take about two days to tell you that whole story ... I mean, *bunch of* stories, sheesh!! For a little taste, stay tuned for the next chapter — The Phil Lesh Story.

But get this — not only did this girl wanna drive from the Cassady Panel to the Cassady Band — but she was staying in frickin' Chinatown!! — so was driving all the way back to about two blocks from where I was staying in North Beach!!!

I dunno, but sometimes the lights all shinin' on me …

Anyway, next thing you know it's **Sunday Sunday Sunday** — the day of the big *"Hitchhiker's Guide to Jack Kerouac"* show. Thank god, ol' Bill-Graham-Jerry moved it to the 4 PM slot so there was time to recover n all.

But first in the day — I mean it was unreal — there was **Jerry doing a show with David Amram** with his usual colorful storytelling and all that jazz. And the authentic rare living Beat poet **David Meltzer** was there doing his funny poetry and mesmerizing storytelling. And there was the great Beat filmmaker **Mary Kerr** screening her movies from North Beach in the '50s. And the artist **Eric Drooker** who did all the animation in the movie *Howl* putting on a whole show. And **Brenda Knight** who did *The Women of the Beat Generation* book among other things — and there was more stuff to do than any one person could.

Plus! **Dennis McNally** was there! — who I still think wrote the best biography of Jack, *Desolate Angel*, not to mention *The Official History of the Grateful Dead*, and he's riffin on the great Wally Hedrick who I'd written about fairly extensively in my *Hitchhiker's* book.

Which led me to meeting this poet / professor, **David Rollison**, who was good friends with Wally, an artist who vociferously shunned the spotlight.

And it was David who set me up on a whole *other* series of adventures just before the Shindig happened — including taking me to the very house I stayed in on the Marin detour in the *Hitchhiker* book, and turning me on to the people who live in the *Dharma Bums* house where Jack & Gary Snyder stayed for a while, and all sorts of other sacred and weird places in Mighty Marin.

And a cool thing had developed by Sunday where this area outside the main front doors became this perpetual groove center — where everybody went in or out . . . but there was me and whomever else at any given time just hangin on the loading dock landing that looped around the entire building — and in a way this was the most fun time and place of the whole Shindig Shabang. Besides our late nights at Vesuvio's, this was the most Beat scene of the summit.

I of course arranged for us to go to the nearest cold beer store and come back with four armfuls loaded for bear. And we could smoke jazz cigarettes in the cool San Francisco Bay breeze, and there was this constant *flow* of people, all of whom would stop for a while, and some of the most interactive subject-leaping conversations of the weekend took place on that stoop. Coulda been New York in the '50s.

There was the great S.F. poet James Stauffer who I finally got to meet after we tried to put together the huge "Holy Fools" festival in the Mid-West about 20 years ago . . . and that colorful Beatific artist Philippo LoGrande from Mexico who's been floating around all conference drawing me and all sorts of other people in the ongoing jam of it all . . . and there was Dan Barth, my Boulder '82 brother, finally with time to hang and groove in poet's grove down by the docks of the city . . .

and there's Tate Swindell and Jerry and Gerd and Levi and James and . . .

... holy shit! — I still have a show to do!

And then this crazy thing happens where — everything had been going perfectly — but sometimes I get these fainting spells where if I don't get horizontal as soon as I feel it coming on, I'll black out and drop like a stone. And sure enough, I hadn't really ate much (or slept much after the Dead Spectacular) and when I picked up a box of books to help somebody move — BOOM it hit! ... And this was 45 minutes before I'm supposed to be "on" — and there I am lying on the floor seeing stars behind the Cassady's table ... !

Way to go, B! You're passing out five minutes before showtime. What? — You trying to pull a Kerouac? I know yer into the guy — but do you really have to be unable to stand before you go on stage?! That wasn't his strongest attribute, I'm thinking, as the ceiling's spinning like a merry-go-round.

I very gradually rise to the occasion, and frailly and slowly make my way to the room with the help of Dr. Wight — and there waiting for me is the unspoken superstar of the conference, Brandon from The Beat Museum setting up to do the visual show with the laptop. And there's a whole room fulla people! ... as I'm one wrong breath away from falling over.

So ... it was a wild trip. But as people noticed, including me, I gradually gained strength as the hour-and-a-half show progressed ... and about half-way through it started to feel like I was coming back. It was cool talking to people afterwards ... that the audience could see this happening ... almost like a Dead show where the first half / set was basically warming up, then the second half killed. I was actually up and running around the stage, and at one point, I don't know what the hell story I was telling, but it required me running across the stage and smashing into the far wall! I have no idea. But I do remember hitting this wall and seeing the paint microscope-close to my eyes and thinking, "Well, I must be feeling better."

41

Anyway, the whole show's on videotape — and this is starting to feel like Steve Goodman's song coming to life.

But at least I was a hundred percent for both Gerd and the Cassadys, and that's what really matters. Honoring your elders and extended family. Which is really what this whole conference was for all of us.

But of course it was no where near over yet!

After my show's done, a bunch of us encamped on the stoop again, and hung there in a most festive space until it got dark, then hung sumore. And then ruth weiss came on to close the conference up in the main theater where we did the Cassady Family show the day before, and we all went up and man, she was great! She had an upright bass, sax, and her partner on a drum, and she read this *very* Beat stuff ... as in, with a beat, the same kind of breath lines as Jack blew, about finding freedom and yourself in a sea of blandness and conformity.

And very cooly, she pulled out all this stuff from her repertoire that dealt directly with Beat subjects — poem-stories about meeting them, and about their lives together back in the day. I know she's continued to write since the '50s, the more recent of which is what she normally performs, but for this Shindig she specially and thankfully selected all her original Beat-based material and quite rocked the house — with more energy than I've seen in performers a quarter her 80 years.

And this was naturally followed by more jazz cigarettes and cold Sierra Nevadas on the stoop while everybody mill-valleyed about, and by now me and ol' Blind Tom had become a somewhat inseparable duo — he was *so* observant — and I convinced him to not leave the next day but stay for the aftershow glow when everyone's relaxed and radiating with the meter off and it's Vesuvio's time.

So ol' Blind Tom wisely does this, and we have a whole day's Adventure . . .

And I'm encouraging him to write up his Shindig story cuz he's about my age when I did the first one and it would be so amazing to read how he perceives *everything* — how he can't see but he's all ears — and the way he so highly functions and learns geography and is so self-reliant and Getting Things Done it's just mind-blowing.

And we happily bop all over North Beach, including hanging with **Paul Kantner** at the vividly historic Caffe Trieste and I tell him about staying in his old house in Marin, and he sits there reading that whole section of my book just like **Phil Lesh** couldn't put it down a week earlier ...

But the coming night was one of those Classics you play for.

It began with the official debriefing hang with the core crew at Vesuvio's — just as I had prophesied to Jerry we'd do months ago — that beaming lingering evening when we're no longer looking at our watches after months of planning and deadlines — Bill & Chet, as he & I started jokingly calling ourselves, honoring the two great San Francisco promoters — and debriefing we did! — including with old show-producing New York partner, Levi Asher .. . taking over the best booth in the best bar in town — right on the street, right in the corner, right under the Kerouac Alley sign, right inside the door, everything wide open and wild!

And off we riffed on the vibe that was pulsating from the opening night party to the closing night stoop; on how so many people met each other for the first time; how Gerd and ruth were like two playful kids even in their 80s; how cool the Prankster presence was and how natural the blend was with the Beats; how effective the big party room was except maybe we should have the poets' stage somewhere else so it's more focused; and how taking over Fort Mason was so perfect, giving us our entire own world in the middle of downtown San Francisco; how glitch-free everything had rolled; and how everybody got home safe.

And suddenly I remembered — "Oh Wait!! There's a super-important scene in my book that takes place here! I sat in here in 1982, right above where we are," I pointed up. "This exact spot, except on the second floor! We gotta go there!" So I Pied Pipered the crew upstairs just before they closed it off for the night, and we took over the very table where me and Croz met that actor! (ch. 27) Another one of those sites from the book I hadn't been to in 33 years!

And after a few more rounds, responsible Bill Graham bids us adieu — and it's pretty much a wrap on the wrap party. And outside in the aforementioned Kerouac Alley, Levi and I have a perfect fare thee well moment, where the giant arc of the rainbow came down just like it did over Levi's Stadium, from East Coast to West, from our first deciding to do this and getting together for the first time in years for this perfect Adventure in Beatlandia, and now the rainbow arc ends in Kerouac Alley between Vesuvio's and City Lights — the bar and the bookstore with Jack the bridge — the only two Shindiggers who did both the conference and the Dead shows hugging goodbye, so much happier than Dean & Sal at their sidewalk farewell in *On The Road*.

And now there were three . . . amigos in the alley . . .

And I figured we had to figure out once-and-for-all exactly where that famous Robbie–McClure–Dylan–Allen photo was taken. And ol' wiz-bang

Brandon pulls out his smart-phaser and beams up
the photograph and zooms in on the doorframe and
a-ha! GOT it! Nailed it. Know it. Now.

So we gotta take the fer-sure pictures in the fer-
sure spot — and so Yes! We reprise the Blind Tom
trick and have him take the photo!

And eventually brilliant Brandon bolts for the
boonies, and I walk my new Brother Tom home —
this Beat conference's Brother Tom, reprising the
real-life character so central to the first one — back
to his Green Tortoise Hostel a half-block from The
Beat Museum — in itself one of the coolest places in
North Beach — a center for off-Beat Travelers and
Adventurers since the mid-'70s.

After the drop-off, I was still way too jazzed n
burnin' to remotely sleep, and there was a whole
city left to explore! Suddenly I was on my own, no
direction home, free to roam under the starry dome.

I hung a right up some little alley next to The
Beat Museum towards The Saloon — since 1861 the
longest continually operating bar in San Francisco
and home to all the desperadoes since Jack London
and Jesse James. Or something. But by now it's
already past the last call for alcohol and they're
not lettin people in the door. But I look closely

and there's ol' Per (pronounced "pair") — my
Danish Deadhead brother who'd flown here from
Copenhagen for the Fare Thee Well shows — and
actually was at the historic Tivoli show on the Europe
'72 tour! We'd been beaming all over North Beach
ever since we both arrived about the same time, and
together we could do a lot of damage.

So I see ol' Per sittin there, and this seems to be
enough for the Wild West Saloon cowboy doorman
to let me slip through the swinging doors, and ol'
Per's just laughing his Danish head off that I found
him, and of course it's time for another Adventure.

We pour outta there, and fall in with this whole
German crew who are similarly prowling The Streets
of No Good, and head round the corner past the
closed Trieste and back out to Columbus where we
got caught up in the whole strip-bar scene with these
hookers and whatevers and guys & dolls of all ages
and ethnicities working the hungry sidewalks for
a mark & a buck, the full-on hustle of end-of-night
scores and hook-ups and tricks and trades and what a
circus!

We linger in the swirling scenery of barkers and
colored balloons — because life is a carnival, two bits
a shot. But then we remember our mission for beer
and continue back to Broadway where the Danes and
Germans hold a curbside summit to determine the
next drinking hole. But it takes this Canadian to break
the news it's a hard 2 A.M. cut-off in this town — and
if Vesuvio's and The Saloon have had last call on a
Monday, there ain't nuthin more late-night than them.

I looked at the deli on the corner and the watch
on my wrist and told ol' Per — "That's the last beer
in town, mate. And it closes in 15 minutes." He
doesn't wanna believe me, so we sit down on these
iron bolted-in bus stop chairs they have, and have a
smoke to think about it, watching the open deli door
as the minutes tick by. And sure enough, since ol'
Per hasn't come up with a better plan, at 1 minute to,
we grab a half-dozen Rolling Rocks, which Per has
some crazy elaborate backstory on about how he
discovered them on some mad mission in America

way-back-when and they hold some special power for him — secret energy juice — and I'll go along with anything for a night.

So we happily load up my road bag and head for my office — this outdoor patio place just down Columbus at Kearny — the perfect setting for the sunset of the trip.

As fate and geography would have it, we had to pass **Specs** on the way — the other historic hideaway bar in North Beach that's been there forever.

I get us to swing left sweet chariot on ol' Saroyan Alley to the tiny bar you'd never know was there . . . unless you did.

And sure as you're born — the door's standing wide open. And as I start to walk in the empty space, the barkeep calls out, "We're closed!"

"Yeah — I just wanna look around" I say, all wide eyed I am — and completely knowing the play I'm playing.

And he lets us wander in . . . and I stay in character . . . the scholarly studious student of history . . . appreciating said bar . . . painstakingly exploring every inch of the framed history on the walls . . .

. . . buying time . . . showing interest . . . while Per goes over and starts talking to the last lingering local at the end of the bar . . . who I actually happen to already know as he's the sometimes doorman at Vesuvio's, the guy who told me how the scene around North Beach had changed so much for the better with the announcement of the Dead shows . . . their first in 20 years . . . and how he, as a street barometer, had noticed a visible change in the hugs and love of strangers stopping strangers just to shake their hand that had been missing for a long time in this Times Square of Bohemia.

And so, with everyone duly occupied, and me tossing out the occasional inquisitive question to the clearly erudite bartender . . . the desired bond seemed to be developing . . . and as the last of the now-drinkless locals wafted out the door . . .

. . . sure as you're born I hear The Magic Words:
"Could you go close that door and lock it?"

BOOM! DONE! *In.* The coolest tiniest
bohemianest bar in S.F. . . . the greatest POSSIBLE
moment and place to be . . . the old The-Bar's-Closed-
And-The-Drinks-Are-Free Routine.

And it turns out this bartender, Michael, is a
doppelganger for the comedian Colin Quinn — accent,
heritage, looks, mannerisms, humor, thoughts . . .

And he re-fills my pint without asking whenever
it's thirsty, and as he's putting everything away
and cleaning up, he says more than once — "If you
were five minutes earlier or five minutes later, this
wouldn't have happened. . . . But you came in *right* in
that window." We both knew the routine, and were
mutually happy to have worked it together.

And boy, was he *smart.* A classical music and
film scholar, he starts playing all these obscure movie
scores that are positively Vivaldian! And as he's
putting stuff away he stops and POUNDS out the
beats on the bar like a teenager does rock n roll —
and fist-pumping the air at the crescendos. The guy
got his B.A. in film, minored in religion and African
studies, and one of the refrains our many-pints-long
conversation keeps returning to is — "respect your
elders." And it was that I respected the history of
the bar that was my pass into this world — as he
reverently tells me about the legendary eccentric
owner nicknamed "Specs" who was a jukebox of one-
liners — "If I'm not in bed by midnight, I go home."

The place is like the original Cedar Tavern or
Kettle of Fish in New York — just a bar — no TVs —
no frills, no nuthin 'cept music and people and drinks
— because what else do you need? I search for the
authenticity in everything — the *real,* the core, the
truth, the root, the undoctored, the natural in both the
outdoors and the indoors — and this place is bona
fide, certified, Beatified *real.*

And after we have this glorious perpetual-pint-
refilling classical music class and North Beach history
lesson, ol' Michael's about finishing his chores, and I
can read the music on the wall and knew this score
was coming to its natural resolution, and knowing not
to overstay our gracious welcome, I suggest to my

Danish Dangerman that we continue on to my office, cuz we've *still* got that 1:59AM purchased six-pack of Rolling Rock to play us through the nocturnal groove-down.

Back on the desolate angel streets of deserted North Beach, America, the only two Beatniks still beating the conversational adventure drums on this sleepy Monday night in June, euphoric in our score of an after-hours bar that looked so impossible when we were last roaming these empty streets of newspapers blowing . . . as we whooshed around the corner to my corner office with a view.

Quite ecstatic in the ecstaticness of the 4AM universe — we've pulled it off! From slipping into the closed Saloon to find him hours ago, to the magic moment in the coolest Kettle this side of 1957, we surfed the waves of this Beach like masters of the never-bored.

And I pulled out my notebook and am readin' him my notes and writin' new ones . . . cuz if there's one thing I've learned it's — you gotta write it when it happens.

As me and Per are taking the talk for one last walk around the track, I know I got work ahead of me.   Gotta get this down. Now.

So we loop back to the hotel weir both staying in and met over Grateful Dead t-shirts in the lobby, and bid each other goodnight.

Now, y'see — when I'm burning, I smoke. And I gotta have a space to write and burn. Normally it's the street — but this is crazy half-lawless North Beach at 4 A.M. When I write, I leave the planet. But one needs to be alert and monitoring the radar systems when you're out in war zones. And I could not leave Earth and be safe with my instrument on the sidewalks of this crazy.

And then — ol' Levi came flashin' back.

Of course, as The Grand Fates had it, I was hanging out front when this brother-from-another-mother arrived to stay in the same joint. And having experienced Brian in New York, Levi asks as I'm walking him to his room, "What's the roof like?"

I say, "There's no way up."

He goes, "Whadda you mean? There's *always* a way up."

Now, A) he's not right about that, but B) the *moment* he says this, we walk past a hallway with a window at the end . . . and a fire escape ladder going up . . . Hmmm . . .

The conversation immediately leapt to another subject, as he and I are wont to do, but the snapshot was logged at CentCom for future reference. "Roger that."

Back to the room — download everything — meaning leave in the room everything you don't need; pack for Adventure: laptop; cold beers from mini-fridge, replaced with the last Rolling Rock; glasses for long range optical enhancement; camera so I can see what we captured from tonight; notebook for retrieval; I.D. because I'm anticipating being caught, and have the whole honest play in my head — "I'm just a writer visiting from Canada and this is my last night, and gosh, I'm sorry, but there were no signs saying you can't take the fire escape to the roof."

BOOM — like Batman, I'm climbing up the side of the building, in the 4AM dark of Big City, America, and sure as shit — it takes you right up!

POW! On the roof! Scout it out. Walk softly and attract no attention.

It's a bit cold, but I'm puckin here! And to prove to anyone maybe watching me from higher buildings, I go and sit and get right to work on the roof hatch cover — the only "seat" on the roof, coming up from a locked room and locked hatch below.

Safe on Heaven's roof.

I'm freaking out that I'm here — but I got shit to do. And I start writing the story you just read. But it's really hard cuz the Coppola Building is hauntingly hovering above me, and Coit Tower's beaconing on the horizon, and Washington Square Church is looming right in front of me . . . and I'm on a roof in North Beach . . . so it's all happening, but I'm forcing myself to get the story down — no hope for full sentences — just exact images — I'll weave 'em

50

together later — as I look around again — surveying the two fire ladder routes to the roof — the only two access points for any enemy (or cop) to appear — and they're both a long way away — as the city lights are painting moving abstracts on the fog — "So *this* is where psychedelic light shows come from!" — and . . . "quit lookin around" — Boom — back to the flashes of story images in sequence — get it down, get it down — even though it's also see-your-breath cold — and see your life-flash-before-your-eyes visual — and the computer screen's fogging with unreadable mist in this rainforest San Francisco Bay moisture — adverse conditions at their best — but write on, muthrbruthr, write on . . . .

And then suddenly — *Oh Shit!* — I'm interrupted by — the pitch black beautiful Sky beginning to turn . . . a smidge off black . . .

"*Oh no* — it's getting light . . . "

Which quickly gave way to ... "*Oh my God!* It's getting light!!"

And thus The Shindig Sutra ends . . .

With a toast to all the new days.

4

Getting My Phil at The Crossroads

It's the Father's Day weekend, 2015, and my bassist bud Al Robinson tipped me that PhilZone. com had its countdown clock to the next Phil show indicating Sunday night. That was the only lead I had.

I was out in the Bay Area where, a few years ago, Phil bought a nice large restaurant and performance space in San Rafael, calling it Terrapin Crossroads. Conferring with my local live music confrère Adrienna, we were able to put the two-and-two together of his son's band, Midnight North, and their Father's Day booking at his father's club, and guesstimated that was the spot.

At the time, I was staying down the coast in the Capitola / Santa Cruz area with the Cassadys, but wanted to do a few days in Marin, so it seemed like Father's Day was the perfect time to transition from Adventures South, to

Adventures North.

I stopped in at John Cassady's in San Jose on the way up, left there about 5:30, and made it to Terrapin Crossroads in San Rafael in an hour and 15 minutes. (!) "You could have been waiting in the line for the [Golden Gate] bridge for an hour and fifteen minutes!" locals later told me, in near disbelief at my Cassady-like road time.

Terrapin Crossroads (TXR for short), is a very large multi-room family-style seafood-leaning restaurant right on the water of the San Rafael harbor, and just a couple blocks from the band's legendary office / rehearsal space on Front St. It has a separate "Grate Room" for larger shows, but every night (and often daytimes too) bands play on a small, low stage in the main restaurant / bar room.

This being 7PM on a Father's Day Sunday there was a long line of people waiting to get in. Having never been here before, I thought they were in line for the Phil concert, and I'm like, "Is this the ticket-holders line?" To which I got strange responses, cuz, see, there are no tickets ... it's a restaurant, you tourist.

The dining tables were all full, but right in front of the tiny stage were a few high bar tables and chairs, and one of them was empty, except for a guy named Cliff. And if you've read *The Hitchhiker's Guide to Jack Kerouac* you know that's a sacred name, a guiding light, in my AdventureLife. Soon weir joined by a guy named Jeff, with this table looking right onto the stage. I asked these regulars if they think Phil is going to play tonight, and they point out there's no big bass rig on the little stage, so they doubt it. "But you never know. We could be sitting here and Phil could come walking right through that door."

And not three minutes after he says this —
here comes Phil walking right through that door
(!) with his wife Jill — and they go sit in a large
open unused area up a couple steps behind the
stage.

I'm kinda freakin out. There he is. The
Man himself. Just a regular dude in a regular
restaurant. About 30 feet away from me.

I've already told Cliff & Jeff about my book
and how I'd love to talk to Phil and maybe give
him a copy.

And pretty much right away, Jill leaves the
table they've encamped at, and as he's just
sitting there, Cliff says to me, "This is probably a
good time to go talk to him. He's all alone. It's
only going to be busier later."

Five minutes earlier it looked like a long-
shot he would be here, and now, with no prep
or no liquid courage to speak of, I was suddenly
"on." It was showtime.

Luckily, blessedly, perfectly — a lightning bolt
across the skull hit me — a-ha — what I could
tell him — how I could start talking to him . . . I
had an angle from an angel . . .

With Coach Cliff pushing me into the deep
end, I grabbed a copy of the book and jumped
off the diving board into sumthin I couldn't turn
back from.

He was sitting with his back to the far wall,
facing into this large unused extra room, and
could see me coming from the moment I crossed
the threshold. I just went for it. Cliff was
right. It was early, things were quiet, and this
was the best shot in what might become a long,
long, crazy, crazy night.

"Hey, Phil."

"Yes," he looks at me, not unfriendly.

"I have a story for ya . . . " I said with a Prankster twinkle, as I dropped down comfortably in a chair facing him. "I just wrote this book about the '82 Kerouac conference in Boulder where you guys played Red Rocks as part of it, and I actually go into the connection between the band and the Beats more than any other book ever, including Dennis's or anybody's," and I've definitely got his eyebrow-arched attention.

"I'm friends with the Cassadys, and was hanging out with Neal & Carolyn's son John a couple days ago — 'Neal's kid' as you guys called him," I said, pointing to him and smiling, and he's nodding yes yes, totally with me. "And ... did you know that *the very last question* Jerry was ever asked on film ... was about Neal?" And he makes this "Wow! I didn't know that!" face.

"John didn't know either, so I read him — rather dramatically — the answer Jerry gave about his Dad, and it was so moving, John actually got choked up and started almost crying. It was unreal."

Here's the part from *The Hitchhiker'Guide ...* I read to John —

In fact, the very last question in the very last interview Garcia ever gave on camera (to the Silicon Valley Historical Association), was about Neal Cassady. "I got to be good friends with him. He was one of those guys that truly was a very *special* person. In my life, **psychedelics and Neal Cassady are almost equal in terms of influence on me**.

"Neal *was* his own art. He wasn't a *musician*, he was a 'Neal Cassady.' He was a set of one. And he was it. He was the whole thing — top, bottom, beginning,

56

end, everything. And people knew it. And people would be drawn to it. He was an unbelievable human being — the energy that he had, and the vocabulary he had of gestures and expressions — oh boy he was funny. Phew! I really loved him." ... were the last words Jerry Garcia ever said on camera.

And John was sitting there shaking with emotion and trying not to totally lose it in front of his friend.

"And *then*, a while later," I keep telling Phil, "Something reminded me of what you wrote in your *Searching For The Sound* which I quoted in my book — you wrote so passionately about Neal — it was so beautiful — so I read John that part — and this time, John started crying almost from the moment I began reading, and so much so, that I started getting choked up ... "

Phil devoted much ink in his memoir to this milestone moment in his life [Neal's death], including, "It hardly seemed credible that a life force like his, so generously endowed with the *rhythm* of motion through time, could be smothered and shut down at such an early age. . . . Neal's death had hit me harder than I knew; I'd been obsessing on the loss of one of the most inspiring people I'd ever known personally. . . . **I vowed to myself that in the future I would live up to Neal's inspirational example.**"

"... and I could barely finish reading it ... and the next thing I know we're in each other's arms hugging and shaking and crying together."

"Wow! That's . . . beautiful!" Phil says, laser-beaming me in the eye. "Thanks for sharing that with me."

"I just thought you should know. ... You wrote

so passionately about Neal ... I thought Johnny should hear it," and we both looked into each other's eyes in a prolonged moment of respect and reflection.

And with that, I gave him a copy of the book, and said Thanks for making the connection to history like he did, and left him to his privacy, as I walked back out of that room, eyes bulging out of my head that this just happened!

Back at the high bar tables in front of the stage, where we had a direct view straight into this wall-less room where I'd just talked to him and the guys had been watching me, I was freaking out. I bought a round for the table in gratitude for their coaching, and I felt like my life was now complete. I'd finally written a book about how the Grateful Dead connect to the Beat writers ... and had passed on copies to both the Cassady family and the main guy in the Dead.

Done.

And as we sat there, eventually I realized, "Geez, I prolly shoulda gotten a picture with him." And ol' Cliff says, "Well, he's still just sitting there. I could take it for you if you wanted." And I looked over at Phil, but he seemed all immersed in something, and I didn't want to disturb him asking a dumb favor. But after a few more moments of reflection and sips of frosty courage, I figured I better do it now — again, while it's early, pre-show, quiet. So I said Yeah to ol' Cliff, "Let's do it."

And as we walked up the couple steps into the extra room where Phil's the only person there, I see he's bent over reading something ... and I'm like, "No! . . . there's no way . . . " And sure as shit — *Phil is sitting there reading my book!* I couldn't believe it!

It certainly made it easy for me to ask, "Hey Phil, can I get a picture with you?"

And he looks up with the biggest smile on his face! "Yeah, sure!" he says with genuine enthusiasm!

And he jumps up for us to do it, then goes, "Wait," and reaches back to the table and grabs the book and holds it up front and center!

Couldn't believe it!

And then the night rolls out, and his son's band plays their first set — a mandolin–electric–guitar bluegrass–rock amalgam with Grate 4-part harmonies — and luckily for all, as a vocalist, the son *did* fall far from the tree — as Pops comes and sits right behind us for the set.

Generally speaking — I'm thinking — "This must be heaven; tonight I crossed the line ..."

I'm just a beaming Brian, floating on the golden road at the end of the rainbow, with a stage-side seat to some fantabulous music, surrounded by new friends, and a photo with Phil on my camera!

Then during the set break, Jill and some other people come and join Phil at their kinda private table in their kinda private room, basically right in front of our field of vision, and I'm sorta keeping an eye on him every few minutes. And then I notice, he's not talking to the other people at the table. He's sitting there, looking into his lap.

"No! . . . No way . . . don't even *think* it … " … but I do. And I get up and go to where I can get a clear view of his lap . . . and sure-a-gawd-damned nuff . . . on Father's Day, with his son's band in the house . . . on a non-work night out with his wife and their friends . . . he's sitting there at their table … *reading my book!*

And then more crazy shit goes down, there may have been some jazz cigarettes involved, and another set of smokin' bluegrass–rock-n-roll, and another round of — get this — Prankster beer!!

And we're talkin at the table about all sorts of stuff including my book, and this other author named Sandy Troy is there, and Merry Prankster Adrienna, and dancin' cowboy Harri, and it's a very High Time with some very hardcore cool Marin County cats, and at some point the jam rolls around to one of the photos on the back cover … from Halloween night, 1980, right after the final Radio City Dead show — and how I only asked to have the picture taken because I'd just found Molson Canadian in a deli for the first time since moving to America a month earlier!

And … I'm actually wearing a Phil Lesh button in the photo!

And then I realize — Shit, I should tell Phil this. He'll never be able to see that that's him on the button. So, sure as heck, being well-primed with some well-placed Prankster beer, I decide to go over one more time — which, y'know, is verging on being a pest. But when I walk up to his now full multiple tables of friends, he looks up, and as joyously as could be, goes, "Oh, hi Brian!" And this is a guy who back in the day had a reputation for sometimes being a little less than friendly to people. But he was just as nice and open and into-it as a person could be.

So I go on one knee beside him with the book on his lap and point to the picture and start to tell him the story about Halloween Radio City, and he goes, "What year was that?" Kinda blew my mind that he played this historic run at Radio City Music Hall, made two double-albums and one movie from it ... and doesn't have a clue what year it was!

Anyway, I tell him the funny story about *why* I had this picture taken and the only reason it exists — because this Canadian was just so jazzed he could get beer from the homeland in New York City — and Phil, being an old Heineken man himself, obviously appreciated a good beer story, and as soon as I told him, he popped his head back and let out a huge laugh, and *totally* got it.

Not only was I not being a pest, but he completely dug why I was telling him this vitally important background.

And then a few days later — while in the middle of another Beat conference — I joined him and 75,000 others at Levi's Stadium, as this beer-and-book-worm played his band's Farewell to California . . . including their song about Cowboy Neal at the wheel of the bus to Never-Ever Land.

Because that's when it all began.

5

Then Along Comes Kesey

Here's an excerpt from *The Hitchhiker's Guide to Jack Kerouac* about first meeting Ken Kesey at the Boulder '82 summit, and his connection to Jack Kerouac.

I was well into Jack — and this whole conference kicked *that* up a few dozen notches — like it did for everybody else — but The Chief and The Boys (the Grateful Dead) — those were the magic beans I wanted to come home with handfuls of.

Kesey (pronounced Key-Zee) had this operating philosophy of having his home address and phone number publicly listed because he didn't want to "pull a Pynchon," as he put it, but rather remain accessible to readers and the rest of humanity. Somehow through the grapevine I'd learned this inside trick before the conference and had actually written him a letter telling him I was coming. What a nut. But I was ballsy, and I've found these happening dudes are way-hip to straight-up good energy. And this was one happening guy I had to meet. (see, also: *Kool-Aid, Electric*.)

Kesey and Kerouac had a lot more in common than just synchronistically sharing the same fiction shelf in every bookstore in the world. In fact, it's almost eerie how similar their lives were.

- They both grew up in low-income working-class households in small towns just outside a major city, not far from the ocean — Kesey in Springfield, Oregon, Jack in Lowell, Mass.
- Both were strong of build and star athletes in their youth — Kesey a champion wrestler and Jack a star running back in football.
- Both got their big break by getting a scholarship or fellowship to the large liberal intellectual city on their respective coasts, San Francisco and New York, and both suddenly found themselves in a small but intense bohemian enclave with other writers who were so good they would become internationally known in their own right — Kesey in the Perry Lane crowd and extended Stanford scene with Larry McMurtry, Wendell Berry, Ed McClanahan, Robert Stone and others, and Kerouac in the extended Columbia scene that soon included Ginsberg, Holmes, Burroughs, Lucien Carr and others.
- Both wrote an unsuccessful first novel about roughly the same subject — small-town boy goes to big bohemian city — Kesey's *End of Autumn* and Kerouac's *The Town and The City* — and with that out of their system both exploded creatively, struck gold, and were forever defined by their second novel — Kesey's *One Flew Over The Cuckoo's Nest* and Kerouac's *On The Road*.
- And in another cosmic karmic twist, just as their surnames appear next to each other on bookshelves, those two defining works are often sequential in alphabetical lists of major 20th

century novels.

- Both books had the exact same champion in the publishing world, and ultimately their editor — Malcolm Cowley — and both were published by Viking Press.
- Both had the same editor years later at Viking-Penguin, David Stanford.
- Both were represented by the same literary agent, Sterling Lord.
- Both ended up writing famous tributes to the other — Viking asked Kerouac to write the blurb for Kesey's *Cuckoo's Nest* ("A great new American novelist.") and Esquire asked Kesey to write the tribute to Kerouac for their landmark "50 Who Made The Difference" Golden Anniversary issue.
- Both were into sparking the sparkling highs of marijuana long before it became popular, and
- Both were involved in a community of artists seeking out mind-expanding drugs before the drugs entered the national consciousness — Kesey & company famously with LSD, and the Beat crew pioneering the search for and experiential reportage on yage, aka ayahuasca.
- And for Men of Letters, both had an uncommonly strong connection to the cutting-edge music of their time — Kesey with the Grateful Dead, and Kerouac with his passion for Bebop, which saw him produce some of the most vivid descriptions ever written about the small-club birth of that idiom.

And . . .

Both were driven by Neal Cassady on the most pivotal road trip of their life.

But one thing Kerouac didn't do was organize large scale

acid parties, and have somebody write a really colorful book about them, and have his house band evolve into The Grateful Dead and light shows and spontaneous street theater and psychedelic art. As Kesey's friend, author Robert Stone, put it, "I feel like I went to a party in 1963 and it sort of spilled out the door and into the street and covered the world"

So, you can see why I was attracted to this particular conference participant, and why I immediately parlayed myself into being Kesey's handler — the guy who was supposed to make sure he was where he was supposed to be.

Good luck with that, kid!

His first event was a big press conference with Allen and Burroughs.

Actually, Allen was at pretty much all of them. Every day we'd have one with a different headliner or two as the focus — Gregory, Burroughs, McClure, Abbie, Leary, etc. — so, over the arc of the conference, whatever day some press person might be covering it, there'd be at least one press availability, with Allen as the omnipresent moderating moderator.

And of course Kesey's late. Way late. I'd called him at the house where he was staying, and he promised they were just leaving. Like — an hour ago.

After much pacing and looking back and forth from my watch to the furthest cars driving in from anywhere near — Kesey finally just "appeared," all alone, blissfully walking up the sidewalk ... a half-hour late. I was quickly learning what was known as "Buddhist time" in Boulder: Things were supposed to happen at a certain time. Unless they didn't.

You're immediately struck by his size and stature, and I don't just mean literary reputation. This was a big man — a wrestler with a tree-trunk neck, a barrel chest, and Popeye forearms; a mountainman with ruddy cheeks and glowing skin; but more impactful than anything was his ever-present smile, his big, easy and infectious laugh, and the Prankster twinkle perpetually flashing in his leprechaun eyes.

"How was the trip here?" I asked.

"Great. We drove 40 hours non-stop," and he turned and smiled a wide one in pride at their Cassady-like achievement. In fact, I'd hear him tell people this for the next week. "All the way from Eu-gene," he'd say, emphasizing the first syllable and not the second, like he always did.

This all sounded well and good and very On The Road and In The Spirit and all that, so I never broke it to the old guy that I got here from Portland, which is *furthur*, in 42 hours — *and I didn't even have a car!* Smoke that in your pipe and hold it.

As we speed-walked the sidewalk to the gig, he also shared, "It was a return trip." I looked at him. "My pa packed up the family and moved us from right near here to where we live now. I was born not far from here. Smack in the middle of the war he up and moved us all to Oregon, been there ever since. But this was my first home."

And then, oh man! **That press conference was sumpthin!** I'll just say straight out — there are very few people I've been around who change a room just by walking into it, but Kesey's one of them. This was just the first of many times I would experience it. It has to do with energy, there's no other way to explain it. People radiate energy, and I saw the effects of Kesey's many times. He'd enter a room, and the whole space would change, even for people who didn't know he was there or who he was. It would get louder and more animated. He was this huge splash in the energy pool, and ripples would roll across the room, hit the far wall, and come rolling back again. Mind you, he was also partnered with his Lieut. Babbs, the former

67

Vietnam helicopter pilot and Senior Prankster who's got a bellowing baritone to match his big Oregon frame. So . . . things change when they walk in a room. As they did to the nines in the Glenn Miller Lounge at this press conference. (And if you hadn't guessed yet — yep, Glenn Miller went to the U of C in Boulder.)

Lined up next to each other were Babbs, Ginzy, Anne Waldman, Burroughs and Kesey in front of the microphones and cameras and tape decks and standing-room-only reporters. The first question was to Kesey, and he was off, galloping with words and thoughts and obscure references, and leaning forward into the questions — not sitting back in his chair — but playing the room, merging the artists and audience like the best musician magicians can do.

6

On The Road
to *On The Road* —
Sex, Drugs & Jazz

A very abnormal thing happens — it's post-
movies Wednesday night when Carolyn Cassady
& I normally part ways for our own offices and
computers, but by fortune we met up in the kitchen
and started talkin about the *On The Road* movie
premiere tomorrow night, and I'm tellin her how
I'm all excited about being in this palace with 2,000
Jack people, but it's sold out, and press is totally
allotted for, and I'm telling her my elaborate plans
for sneaking in, or scoring a ticket out front, but
that I *have* to be there, and suddenly she's, "Well,
I should write you a letter to get in. I wanna know
what you think of it."

And I'm like, "Yeah."

And she's like, "Okay, I'll do it now," and I hand
her a pad & pencil and she writes out a late-night
plea for me to get into this thing as her eyes & ears
since she can't make it.

And then, by the time I get up in the morning, she's handwritten a whole new killer "letter of introduction" for me to carry with as the revised Plan A!

So I go in to London from Bracknell. But problem is: the last train back out tonight is at 11:38PM — about the time the movie's ending. This is gonna be dicey. So, I time myself from the station. It's 2:10PM at the Waterloo train platforms . . . and 2:17 when I'm at the doors to Somerset House — the palace where the film is to screen in the outdoor courtyard. 7 minutes speed-walking.

I do a thorough pre-scout for getting-in plans B thru D, but have to remember it's Plan A that must work and solve all. So I go to reception thinkin I can get somebody from the film fest to come down and between the letter and me, convince 'em to let me in. But reception says, No Go. You gotta take any delivery to the messenger center, which is outside, down around the corner, down a dark dingy alley that hasn't been cleaned since before the war, and it's spooky old New York. And I get to the end of the dark tunnel where my letter's goin nowhere, but then I bump into the messenger crew. And all my life, including all my years at MTV, I could groove and work with the top executives and have all the mailroom guys love me too. And so Boom — I'm back in Mailroomville, and groovin with the cats, and we're talkin New York and New Orleans, and Assam is right into helping me, and brings me two different envelopes to choose from to put my loose letter in, and says he'll take it right up.

I walk outta the dark tunnel back into the glorious sun over the Thames with the breeze and river air and head back to reception where I said I'd wait, and get up there and I know there's gonna be nothing happening for gawd nose how long, so I go out on the terrace overlooking the airy river, and no sooner am I out there than I see Assam again! And he's already dropped it off and says they'll come find me in reception. "Okay!" So I go back in, plop myself down on a comfy, pull out my Bible — the scroll version — and am just gawkin' around when I see a smiling face seem to pick me out of the crowd. "Are you Brian?" she asks as I notice she doesn't have a ticket in her hand.

"Hi," I stand up.

"We'd love for you to come tonight," she says in the cutest English accent I ever did hear!

And I walk outta there at 3:10, an hour after I landed, with my name on the guest list!

So the next problem to solve is the departure — and having beers for the post-movie writing thinking train ride home. I wanna be (close to) straight for the movie, but afterwards I wanna celebrate. And I check every store on the block and of course in this godforsaken regressive country you can't even buy beers to go after 11. So, whaddya do?

Me, I go back into the venue and start talkin up the cool bar manager at the only bar inside as they're setting up. I explain my situation. She's sympathetic. And I'm like, "Kay, what if I paid you for two beers now — cuz I know you'll be closed at T minus D-hour — and you keep 'em on ice, and I'll grab them as I'm running out the door for my last-train-outta-Dodge." And she winks, and says,

71

"Cool."
Done.

Next: Make the scene. This is a one-time-only gig. In a big cobblestone courtyard of a 450 year old palace. Oh yeah, so I buy one of the padded blankets they sell there, which turned out to be a total savior, turning the ancient London cobblestones into a soft field. And I start talkin to all these girls. And this is the whole bloody point. There's TONS of 'em! I mean, *mostly* girls. I mean, *way* mostly girls. Like, at the start of the line goin in, there was maybe 5 dudes in the first 40 people. !! The total opposite of what we've always thought to be the Beat audience.

And I'm talkin to them and a bunch of them say *On The Road* is their favorite book! Huh?! Crazy, man.

And funny — Kerouac and Keith — you'd see these globetrotting hipsters coming through the portico into the open courtyard, and a very easy smiling question was, "You here for *On The Road* or the Stones?" whose 50th year photo retrospective is also in the same palace at the same time. The Rock & The Road. *Sympathy For The Dharma*. *19th Nervous Beatnik*.

After first scouting the empty yard for where I wanted to experience it from — dead center, really close — I meet up with this girl I'd met literally last night on Facebook, and we're yakin, and she's near the front of the now really long line — in fact there were *two* really long lines "queuing" to get in.

I now know the security search routine — so I pick the fastest guy and the shortest line, and Boom suddenly I'm one of the first people in the naked courtyard, and just Zoom myself right to exact Dead center. And then all the girls catch up and I end up in the middle of this crew of 12 of them! and everything's rollin right along.

And so we're rappin the universe, and how they love the adventure of Jack's books, and the language it's written in, and the openness, and the road adventures — and not only is this crew *from* all over, but they *travel* all over!

And we're yakin an' jammin an' yeah-manin, and the whole time over the crystal PA they're playing this *great* '40s & '50s jazz for the two hour party before the movie, and then — "Oh — there's Al Hinkle!" Or at least the guy who plays him in the film. He's no big movie star, and he's not in it or the book that much, well he is, but he's not that vocal, but he's totally THERE, and pretty much the only other guy on the bus. And Carolyn remained really close friends with the Hinkles throughout the decades & madness they all lived through and I've recently gained a lot of respect for survivor Al — the only major character On The Road besides Carolyn who's still alive.

So I walk up to the actor — "Al Hinkle! I know you!" And he starts beamin' while processing, "Not only does this guy recognize me, and not only as the part, but as the guy behind the part." And we're talking about him meeting Al at the wrap party in S.F. and what a nice and still cogent guy he is, and how he taught the cast how to do the benzedrine inhalers, which they got firsthand-right in the movie, and of course we snap a snap in the crazy courtyard

of some King of Somerset or whoever this palace
was built for.

   Oh, and before the screening a few of the actors
came out for a little interview segment, and Al /
Ed Dunkel, actually Danny Morgan, said, "I don't
really know why I'm here, I'm barely in the movie.
I actually only did the catering on this." Then the
host says, "Well, when Danny comes on screen we
should give him a big round of applause." Then the
movie starts and everyone gets sucked right in, but
about a half-hour later when Al / Ed / Danny gets
his first scene a whole bunch of us remember and
this silly applause breaks out all over the courtyard.
   And, man, here's the crazy part — we're
seeing On The Road ... **at a drive-in movie
screen!!**
   Except there's no cars — it's blankets instead.
But we're outside with this giant screen and the
breeze is blowin and people are munchin on
munchies and they've brought on any manner of
pillows and bedding and picnics and boxed wine, and
there's gay encampments, and loving hetero couples
on pillows, and passels of girls like this is some chick
flick.

And speaking of that — Kristen Stewart
definitely wins the Most Improved Character From
The Novel Award.

Okay, so here's the thing about the movie:

On The Road is only the skeleton this film is
fleshed out around. It is not simply the novel
made into a movie. Director Walter Salles and
screenwriter Jose Rivera WAY expanded it. For
starters, they used The Scroll, not the '57 edition
as the working blueprint. And then all sorts
of little touches were added from Neal, Jack &
Allen's letters, Carolyn's book, the two different
LuAnne interviews, *The Town And The City*, Jack's
audio recordings and articles and notebooks,
Allen's *Denver Doldrums, Dakar Doldrums,* and
the *Martyrdom and Artifice* journals, John Clellon
Holmes' *Go,* and Gifford & Lee's *Jack's Book* — all
noticed specifically. In other words, there's a lot of
stuff that's not in the novel. But it's all based on
firsthand accounts, not solely *Jack's* account as told
in that one book, scroll or not.

And it also does not tell the novel
chronologically. It jumps around — not in a bad
way, cuz it's all part of The Grand Duluoz Legend,
and it's all different refractions of the same light —
but it's not the novel *On The Road* as a linear film.
It's an interpretation based strongly ON that novel,
but it's not a literal filming of the storyline. It's a
work of art, its own work of art, a new work of art

based on an old work of art.

There's lots of cool things about it. I don't want to "spoil" it for you, but many of the specific scenes in the novel that always stood out for me are in the film. And since it's so non-linear, you don't know what's coming next. And it's, "Oh wow! It's this scene! No way!" It's so funny-cool that way. Something that Jack might spend a couple paragraphs on in a 300-page novel could be 3 minutes of the 137 minute movie. And things he might cover over 20 pages aren't included at all. It's kind of a series of choice scenes portrayed.

And the cameos by Terrence Howard and Steve Buscemi are to die for! That two of my favorite actors are in this in such weird and wonderful ways is just great.

And Viggo as Bill Burroughs! Holy shit. Maybe the best part of the film.

And the music is GREAT. Yer gonna love it if ya love it.

There's some problems, big and small, but I'm not gonna mention 'em cuz maybe you won't even notice 'em. It's its own work of art, its own statement, its own piece. It's new and different and will stand (or fall) on its own. But the movie of *On The Road* now exists. And here it is. It's more large than small. It's more new than old. It's more timeless than dated.

How this is gonna play for other people will be interesting to see. But here's a wild example . . .

So, I gotta leave — it's this whole trip. I time it out during the pre-movie layabout. Gotta be on the Strand by 11:30 to get a cab to the 11:38 last-train-outta-Waterloo. I need 5 minutes to find the bar manager and grab those road jars. It's gonna take 5 minutes to get from where I am in dead-center of Woodstock to that bar. Plus a 5 minute buffer. No matter what's happening in the movie — I gotta move at 11:15.

So, I execute the exit — and my girl's in her

closed bar with my two giant beers on ice like champaign. And I see the great final shot from the tunnel leading to the street while walking backwards, then turn around and run out onto the Strand but it's late night Nowheresville in London and there's no freakin cabs! Then I spot one but he cuts down a different split in the road, so I run across the street to where he's heading and there's this moped thing they all ride here right in front of me and with my left hand I'm circle-waving him to keep going past while my right hand is stretched out back flagging the cab. Perfect execution. In the door. "Waterloo Station."

I'm thinkin I'm making good time, get to the steps under that great statue still thinkin I'm doin' good, but look at watch and it's 11:36! Bolt up the stairs nearest the platform the train always leaves from but for some reason tonight it's at the other end of the freakin station! So I jog the entire length of Waterloo Station through the crowds, then fly through the gate, flash-confirming I'm getting on the right train.

You come in at the back of the train and of course all the seats are full, so I'm speed-walkin past it and luckily look up ahead and see Neal the brakeman starting to wave his flag and flash his flashlight just before he blows his whistle, and I go, "Shit," and jump on, and before I'm out of the

doorway the doors close! 5 seconds to spare! 10 if
ya count that first door I walked past. Yet another
close last-train exit execution!

And of course there's no seats! Like, why don't
you run another frickin train after this one? Their
economy sucks, and they force everybody to close
up shop at 11:00! I don't get it. Like, how old are
children who have to be in bed by 11? Does this
country not think adults live here?

Anywho, I walk through the *entire* train ... all
the way to the end of the very front car to find the
very last seat. Sit down, all crazy. I'm five minutes
out of the movie, five seconds from missing the last
train, and I've got an hour to write, and two frosties
to drink. Perfect. I'm write into it. Then after a
few stops the nice woman next to me starts pickin
up her stuff to get off, so I break from my reverie
and say, "Were you in at something good in London
tonight?"

And the woman goes, "Oh, I was just at this
outdoor film *that went on and on.*"

Thousands of passengers leaving on hundreds
of trains and I sit beside someone who was at the
premiere!! "Wait a minute — were you at Somerset
House?! *So was I!*" And we have a little "how
funny!" as she's standing up to get off — but the
point is, she didn't say, "I was just at this great
movie."

There's gonna be the Beat world's reaction, and
then the non-Beat world's. Beat people in general
are gonna like it — cuz it's *On The Road* and so
much more — with a well portrayed Allen and Bill
as well as Neal & Jack. People who have only read
the one book and have it emblazoned in their brains
may have trouble with how it's been expanded, or
edited by the limitations of the medium. I have no
idea how non-Beat-familiar people will respond. Not
a clue. I think if you were predisposed this way,
you'd already be there.

Oh, and there's *a whole lotta* sex in it. The

things that are said and the things that are shown, for The Puritanical American Rating System, this is gonna be an "R" fer sure. I mean, there's hand-jobs, oral, gay, straight, three-ways, you name it — and f-bombs! which actually were not in the casual vernacular of the time the way they're used in this film, and certainly not in the novel. This is definitely an adult movie. Which, if you know your *On The Road*, was a pretty G-rated book, other than the subject — the sex is all off-page, and the language is clean. The movie — not so much.

I look forward to experiencing this many more times, under many different circumstances, in many different mindframes, with many different people, and how it'll continue to reveal new colors and angles with each new Road adventure. It's a memorable, expansive dramatization. It's a helluva party condensed into two hours. It's a road trip with old friends to familiar places. But you better leave the book at home and be ready for anything.

7

Making Better Time
On The Road

So, I get to the Ryerson Theatre in Toronto at 7PM for a 9:00 show and there's already a whole scene. It's the World Premiere of the new *On The Road* — the first-ever screening of the director's revised and final cut.

There's a line of black VIP shuttle cars. News trucks with their satellites up. Fans behind barricades. A red carpet. Security. Orange-shirted volunteers by the bucketful. And a line that goes all the way down the street and around the corner. And same as the London premiere — there's way more yin than yang.

So, I'm scouting it as usual, and the long and the short of it is, I end up weaving my way into the photog's pit along the red carpet. And I start talkin to this girl from the *Daily News* — yeah, New York! And along the ground under the rope line are these numbers about one foot apart and that's where each news person gets to stand. And we're hangin, and as it gets closer to "showtime" I realize nobody's really been stepping on the number right next to

81

her, so I do! And now I'm number 28 along the rope with some TV show called *Red Carpet Diary* on my other side. Then suddenly this stern-faced female General appears marching down the line in front of us demanding the platoon of every soldier. I blurt out, "RockPeaks and LiteraryKicks," and she goes "Okay," and keeps movin' on to the next guy. :-0

So there I am, leaning on the glad-handing rope-line as director Walter Salles and movie stars Garrett Hedlund, Kristen Stewart and Kirsten Dunst work it!

And they end up staying out there a really long time alternating between interviews and answering the screams of fans on the other side — signing autographs and posing for pictures and totally workin' the room. Turns out they were having technical projector problems inside that were being worked out, so they just had the stars stay out with some slight-of-hand distracting.

And of course my road brother Damo's found me by this point and he too scams his way into the photog pit on the rope-line like the magician he is. Then he's the one who spots they're finally letting people into the theatre behind us, a cue we've been watching for, and we've had enough face time with *People Magazine* so we book it into the room and scootch right up to the Reserved Seats, and I notice there's a two-spot Reserved on the aisle right behind the main taped-off rows. Thought that looked interesting — so we cop the two next to them, and no sooner do we sit down, than James Franco comes and sits right next to me!

This guy was the greatest Ginsberg ever on film in *Howl* and I tell him so. "You're gonna go places — *I predict!*" And he's got this great laugh and smile, even though he's all slouching down in his seat and wearing a baseball cap and looking like a scraggly skateboard bum so as not to be recognized. And I ask, "How come you're not in this?" and he says they talked about it but it just never worked out. And I'm opening smuggled beers and takin' copious notes and he's laughin n noddin at crazy compulsive-efficient Brian.

And of course the place is packed and it's a bit of a wonderfully boisterous late-show TIFF premiere audience, and director Walter Salles comes out for a little howdy-do. He talked quite accurately about this city being one of the great film capitals of the world, not only in the making of films but in the sophistication of filmgoers, and how he was so grateful to have this film debuting to this audience. He talked about how the film was partially shot in Canada and how it was very emotional for him to be back here now. And about how everyone on the crew were co-authors of the film. And how they covered 60,000 miles in the making of it in order to get the right locations. Then he quoted Gary Snyder as telling him one day, "We would drive a thousand miles for one good conversation."

Then the preview shorts start and the audience
is cheering or booing or laughing at the little ads.
And one comes on for this James Bond exhibit
they're having at TIFF, and as it ends to dead
silence, some guy yells, "Come on, it's James Bond,
people!!" and everyone laughs and applauds. And
then some little notice appears about copyright
infringement and everybody boos. And I'm thinkin,
"This is a great audience!"

Okay, so . . . the new version —

It's totally different, and totally great!

The entire prior opening scene with the funeral
of the father is scrapped, and it's just BOOM right
into Dean parking cars in New York. And then zoom
into the West End Bar with Chad King telling Sal and
Carlo that this guy from Denver was in town.

You would have liked the longer version — but
you're gonna *Love* this version!

It's way faster paced, way more focused, way
more fun, and way more exciting.

It's more about the writer's journey of discovery
of his voice and vision and less about all the side
stories. It's more Tom Wolfe than Thomas Wolfe

— more poetic zip, less prosaic lag — more broken Benzedrine inhalers and less counted coffee spoons.

The first time, I was so busy following the story and the novel and all the sources and *thinking* — this time I was more open to the incredible landscapes, visages, car shots, and time-period time-travel. You're so there, 1947-to-50 New York City – San Francisco – Denver – and *on the road*, baby. And for instance there's this killer shot of a misty mountain roadside and you can hear Jack singing his roadsong, and before long out of the white nothingness comes Jack amblin' along, rucksack on back.

And Garrett Hedlund really does give a pretty darn good performance. I guess because we know the main characters so well, and Marylou was such an enigma, that Kristen Stewart's character really screamed to life for me the first time I saw it. With that now internalized — I was able to appreciate how electric and magnetic this Hedlund guy was as Dean.

And Tom Sturridge who plays Carlo is similarly engaging. I don't know how Allen actually moved or spoke in the 1940s, and I don't think this is really him, but it certainly is a vivid, loveable, endearing Carlo.

And the music is GREAT — the soundtrack is seat-bopping, and the surroundsound was booming! And the original music that runs all through it is super percussive (beat) and catchy and gets-ya-goin' and I love it!

And there's more voiceovers by the narrator-writer Sal, heard as moody remembrances of things past or excited updates on events present.

There's no point in, or really way to, annotate all the things that were cut, because sometimes it's just a line or few seconds of a scene. But then there's all this stuff added, too — like Dean & Carlo on the bed staring into each other's eyes and more, and this whole coda after the movie's over that I won't tell you about, but it wasn't there before, and is very effective.

During the first viewing I noticed how much sex there was in it. This time I noticed they seem to be smoking joints in just about every scene!

And yeah, you Beat junkies, me included, are gonna wanna have both versions on DVD. They *are* two different Road trips.

When the film was over, TIFF Director Piers Handling came out with Walter, Garrett, Kirsten and Kristen — to huge applause, and screaming, actually — for about a 15 minute Q&A.

86

Walter talked about reading the book as a teenager in the 70s in his native Brazil when it was under a strict military regime and there was censorship and this book represented all the things they were being denied at the time — "where all forms of freedom were possible. And it stayed with me for many many years. In fact, before making *The Motorcycle Diaries* I read *On The Road* again because I wanted to be inhabited by the beauty of that transition between youth and adulthood. It was both what it was telling me, but also how it was written."

Garrett Hedlund (Dean/Neal) was asked about his research and once again went on about how great it was to meet the Cassadys! "Making this movie was a wild journey, a wild life experience — being such a fan of the Beat Generation and Neal Cassady. And then being blessed to meet John — Neal and Carolyn's only son — and being able to ask him every question I wanted and hear his stories about his dad. And meeting Michael McClure, and Carolyn Cassady in London, and to get to know this man through the letters and unpublished writings, it was so rich, learning about this person who inspired me so much, and so many others — other Beat writers, rock stars, people who were lost and wanted to go on their own journey to find something much greater than themselves."

Kirsten Dunst (Camille/Carolyn) — "I read Carolyn's book, and even though she didn't love his lifestyle, I think at the end of the day, she really wanted 'them.' And she gave up a lot for this man, but sometimes 'love' takes you places you wish you didn't go, to deeper selves. She was very enveloped in this man's life. She got the short end of the stick in a way, but had the life that she wanted at times."

Kristen Stewart (Marylou/LuAnne) — "The big question I had going into this was: How did she have the capacity to handle what she handled and still have the life she had that influenced so many people and not have the light go out inside her? And . . . *bottomless pit* — that's the answer! There was no end to her giving. She would have been essential now. I know it's taken a long time to tell the story in film, but she was ahead of her time, and even now, she's really relevant. She had such an acceptance of others. I feel I got to know her so well that whenever I got nervous and wondered if I was doing her justice, not only did I just have to look up to Walter to know, but mostly I would look up and she was so so so fucking looking over me."

And the Q&A ends, and the cast & directors exit stage left, and all along I'm thinking I'm totally fine with just being at the premiere, and already had the red carpet surprise, and hadn't arranged for any after-party, and Walter or the cast never came and sat near us, and now they'd disappeared behind the Wizard's curtain, and people were leaving the theater, and I was cool with it all.

But still, Damo and I are telepathically plotting our next non-leaving nefarious move, knowing where the rainbow came down and the pot of gold was hiding. Except there were security guards at the stairs to both screen-side backstage entrances.

Each of us at different times made a motion to give up and leave, but the other always made a counter-move to keep it goin', keep hangin' on for one last opening, letting the crowd disperse. And before too long it was pretty much only the TIFF staff cleaning the theater and it's all dark and no one's there, and all of a sudden I notice the guard at the door the cast exited through was leaving! Ah-ha! I watch her walk all the way up the aisle, and I'm, "This is it. I'm goin'," and I just walk up the stairs like I live there, push the door, and it swings open! And I see a bunch of people in fancy suits down the hall.

Onward!

Boom! There's Walter and Garrett and Kirsten and company!

A little awkward at first. We're bustin into the dressing room, and nobody knows us. I think of a question about that new final coda scene, but as I'm starting to talk to Kirsten about it, the publicity people call out, "Kirsten, your car's ready." So that ends quickly. Then I start to ask Garrett the same question, *and the same thing happens!!* And now all I'm left with is Walter! And he's talking to the Director of the Festival. But I'm stickin right there and making my presence known. And both of them look at me like, this guy's not goin' away. Because also, I don't want that car annoucement to happen again!

So finally they start to slightly separate. There's a pause and a glance, and I'm, "Hey Walter, I'm Carolyn's friend who was with her this summer in England."

And thus begins ... a whole new adventure ...

Big smile. "Oh, man! I've heard so much about you!" And we start talkin and sure enough right away the car call comes. And he's like, "Okay, we're going to the party. Would you like to join us?"

"Hold on, lemmi check my schedule."

And he puts his hand on the small of my back, saying in gesture, "Come on, you're with me."

And we walk out the stage door and it's that scene I've only seen on screens, where you're in the quiet inside backstage space and the 2 doors suddenly swing open to the screaming barricaded-off fans packing the sidewalk, and flashbulbs going

off, and people reaching out with things to sign
and calling, "Walter! Walter!" And James Franco's
comin' out right behind us and they're yellin' at him
too. And I stand center carpet as they each stop
and sign a few things quite politely, and give legible
signatures and all.

And then it's into this spaceship SUV stretch
limo, and Walter gets in the row right in front
of Damo and me, and leans over the seat and
totally zooms in on us for the whole car ride even
though there's all these other (important) people in
there. And right off we're talkin' Mississippi Gene
and other brief-mention minutia with ease. And
Boom I tell him how great the Slim Gaillard guy
was! And he says he was the #2 man in Kid Creole
& the Coconuts, and how the guy (Coati Mundi)
improvised his whole musical performance.

I asked him what his motivation was in making
the new version and he said he was trying to focus
more on the friendship between Sal and Dean.
And we're talking about the editing process — and
he's quoting the French poet Valery — "A poem is
never finished, only abandoned" — as we riff on a
mutual love of tweaking, and how the scroll had all
those penciled corrections on it, and all the other
versions that came later, and we're having this long
nodding mutual-understanding conversation about
the powers and joys of editing — while we're at the
celebration of Mr. Spontaneous Prose.

And we talked about how great it is to see
the scroll in person, and how the guy who's its
caretaker, Jim Canary, is the coolest, and Walter
says with a laugh he looks like he's in ZZ Top.

And he talked about how the audio mix took a
long time, and I told him how great it sounded in
the house, and cited the psychedelically surreal Sal-
sick-in-Mexico scene — and he and I both said the
word "dizzying" at the same time.

Then I said, "Man, you did so much research,
you so internalized everything, how come Sal's not

using the spiral nickel notebooks?"

And he said they used "both schools" of notebook, the spiral and the flat-topped, and it just turned out that all the scenes with the spiral got cut, and the scenes with the flat-topped made the final.

And we're talking about the changed opening and how the flatbed truck scene is back in the sequence where it belongs, and I ask him about that hokey line he cut from the long version that wasn't in the book anyway — "Are you goin' someplace or just goin?"

"I guess I'm just goin."

And he says it *was* in the book.

And I say, "No it wasn't. And I've got *The Scroll* right here," and start to pull the book out of my bag, and he goes, "No, it's not said on the flatbed, it's from somewhere else in the book."

Ah-ha.

Which is just another confirmation of how this is pieced together from stuff all over the book and elsewhere in order to tell the cinematic story.

I asked him about the cutting of the "respectability" line and the post Camille kicking Dean & Sal out scene with her getting ready for work the next day, and he said that Carolyn had pointed out she wasn't a nurse and so it wasn't perfectly accurate anyway, and that he was trying to zip the movie along and that was something that could be cut.

Eventually we get to the party, and there's this whole scene out front of this new club that hasn't opened to the public yet, and again I get the hand-to-the-small-of-the-back routine as he pushes me ahead of him behind the red velvet ropes. I knew all along the only way I was getting into this afterparty was with somebody from the movie, but never dreamed it would be with the director!

And then as soon as we go behind the lines there's another one of those photo-op backdrops

and a line of photographers behind another
rope, and they're yelling "Walter! Walter!" and
he says, "Okay, *take me with these guys*," and
enthusiastically grabs me on one side and Damo
on the other and the three of us stand there arm-
in-arm beaming like Road Buddies just back from
a trip and joyous and crazy and flashbulbs goin off
like mad with those cameras that shoot pictures
clicketty-click-click-click 20 shots in 10 seconds,
zippity doo-dah, snap-snap-snap.

Then we walk into the mob of a party, and
Walter leans to my ear and says, "You know the
trick with these things? You stay for 8 minutes."
And suddenly the publicity handlers are urgently
saying, "Walter, we have to get you to your spot
upstairs." And I spy this stairway on the other side
of the room so I actually lead the crew through
the crowd and up the stairs to the private party
overlooking the main floor. And there's the lady in
white again, Kirsten Dunst, and the producers from
Zoetrope and MK2 and all these other happening
movie people.

And the crazy thing is, we're there about an
hour, and he and I talk for about 45 minutes of it!

I'm sure one key to us connecting was that I knew this was not a movie about Jack and Neal, but about Sal and Dean, and how we were always talking about the characters and not the biography.

It's a total replay of when I first met my ultimate hero Bill Graham backstage at a Santana concert in New York when I was about 19, and he and I fell right into this intense conversation about the philosophy of show production, and I could see out the corners of my eyes all these people standing there wanting to talk to Bill who is ignoring them all and just locked in on me as we philosophized for the longest with this crowd of burning eyes surrounding us but neither giving any quarter.

And so Walter and I just riff, nose-to-nose about an inch apart, both to hear and cuz it's so crowded. And I ask him everything I can think of.

Right away we talk about the different versions of course, and how people are already writing on IMDb and elsewhere about wanting to buy the longer "director's cut," and I know what he's gonna say, and he says it — "They're both director's cuts."

And he tells me the longer version is for sale in France and the dialog is Not overdubbed, it just has subtitles that you can turn off. And the shorter one will be out on DVD in North America next year.

I told him the new version was the single, and the other was the album version, and he beamed like Scotty.

And I mentioned how I loved the prior opening he cut where it was Sal singing the *On The Road* song from the Kerouac audio recordings (Rykodisc 1999) and how the screen slowly fades from black into Sal's feet walking along the dirt road. And he smiles and twinkles and says he loved that, too. He didn't say it, but we both know Faulkner's lesson — kill your darlings. And he practices it on a big screen big scale budget. Sometimes you gotta cut your favorite passage for the betterment of the story.

And I asked if there was going to be another edit, and he confirmed that No this was it.

And then some voluptuous blond VIP waitress in a form-fitting black mini-skirt comes around and asks if we want anything, and Walter has his water and says no, but I ask for a beer — and it turns out the party is sponsored by Grolsch! And she brings me one of those big wonderful freezing cold bottles with the resealable cap.

Road jar!

And I asked him if anybody else was at both the long-version London premiere and the short-version Toronto premiere, and he thought a second and said, "Yeah, two people. One of the producers ... *and you*," and pokes me in the chest and smiles another crinkly-eyed beauty.

So I start telling him all about the outdoor Somerset screening scene he missed and Carolyn's classic "letter of introduction" and how people brought their entire bedrooms and set them up in the piazza and how it was like seeing *On The Road* at a drive-in except people had blankets instead of cars, and he's just beaming like a proud father at the visual recreation of his film's U.K. premiere.

And we got talkin about the purity of interpreting the book, and he was sayin how the novel was free-form, the spirit was free-form, the life was free-form, and so the movie should be as well. And I'm nodding Yes, and chanced a quote from my London review, "It's a helluva party condensed into 2 hours. It's a road trip with old friends to familiar places. But you better leave the book at home and be ready for anything." And he says, "Yes, that's exactly it."

And we kept riffin' on the improv, and he tells me about the older Okie hitchhiker who sings the song about *"we were once friends,*
but it's hard when you're burning in hell,
and it's hard enough to be in love,
and it's hard, ain't it hard to love what you kill,"
that resonates so painfully with Marylou, and he

94

tells me that whole scene was improvised by the actor who just started singing in the backseat of the car, and that he's an old Kerouac-head and knew the stuff inside out. But can you believe this guy got a bit part in the movie and then created a whole new scene on the spot that made the final cut?!!

I asked him if the *In Search Of On The Road* doc he's been making for years with scads of interviews and Road research would be a separate release and he said that's the plan ... whenever he can get the time to finish it.

And he went into a riff about how the Beats were the catalyst for everything, and I asked if he'd seen *The Source*, and he rhymed, "Of course," as we harmonized on how perfectly inclusive and expansive that doc was.

And we talked about the sex scenes, and he said, "Yeah, you can tell Carolyn there's less now," and we both smiled. And he goes on about how great her writing still is, even in emails. And I say, "Yeah, and she's still a flawless touch-typist," and act out what she looks like typing away with all ten fingers while staring off at her giant Mac screen. And he goes into how much he loved her introduction to *Neal's Collected Letters*, how she describes how painful it was for her to read all those letters, but that she included them all to present the full picture of Neal and let others see for themselves the most accurate *portrait* (like she used to paint).

And I brought up how I thought the casting was great, and he must be so happy, but how did he come to choose Sam Riley?

He said he tried out 200 Sals!! And he picked Sam because he could *listen* — that a big part of Sal is taking in what's around him. He said James Franco tested for it five times and he's great but it just didn't work.

And then we fell into this whole talk about friendship, and how Jack and Neal drifted apart, and how that was such a sad part of the novel, and Walter told me he cried when he first read it as a young man. And then he went off on a parenthetical about how much he loved John Clellon Holmes' *Go* and how Jack's character and friendships are portrayed there. And I told him about my three months of Camp Carolyn dispatches, and how one of them was a riff on friendship, and losing it, and how it can be so intense and then can be so gone. And he's nodding, "Yes, yes," and saying it's happened to him with friends in his life and that he understands and it's sad but it's life.

And I asked him about the dropping of f-bombs, and how that word wasn't in the novels or letters or anything, and he understood my raising it, but that he felt they were little cues that he could use that would connect the story with a contemporary audience, that it's not a documentary, and that they were used very judiciously, and he's right. (But I'll tell ya, the period sets and costumes and cars and locations are all transportively real!) And he said that in *Motorcycle Diaries* he also inserted stuff that wasn't literally accurate for the time because it could help connect an audience in the present.

And we talked about the Jack & Carolyn dancing scene in Denver, and I asked about the famous line that's not in the movie, when Jack said to Carolyn about Neal seeing her first, and he said that it wasn't in the novel, and that he showed their love without using the words, and I'm thinking, "Boy, you sure did" — the attraction's so evident in the faces in that scene.

And there's this great moment where I say, "Oh wait — I'm mad at you!" And I see his wonderfully wrinkling eyes scrunch up and white teeth shine through the darkness. "The San Francisco epiphany scene after Dean abandons Sal & Marylou out there — that was so much more flushed out in the longer version — the picking up of butts from the sidewalk, hallucinating his mother's face in the store window ..." And Walter's smiling and says, "Yeah, I loved

that, too … but I was trying to make it shorter."
 "Why?"
 "Cuz if we could get it down to 2 hours then
theaters can run 4 screenings a day instead of 3.
It's gives it more of a chance and longer theater life.
It's good for the film."
 And he introduced me to the guy from Coppola's
Zoetrope who was the person who first connected
On The Road to Walter — and boy did I thank him
for that!
 And we talked about the rollout and how it was
going to all these film festivals first to have proper
cinephile debuts in different countries all over the
world. He started listing them all but I couldn't
keep track and hadn't heard of half of them.
 And he confirmed that the release dates and
rollout stuff was not his thing, and he put up his
hands saying something like, "That's not my dept. I
just leave that to them."
 And I complemented his choice of no title in the
beginning — it just starts "New York, 1947" and
Boom you're right into the movie and *on the road*,
and he twinkled, knowin' he'd played the solo sweet.
 And I mentioned how poetically beautiful the
landscape shots were and he said they shot those
on a long second unit trip across the country
afterwards.
 And I told him how great Viggo was as Bull/Bill,
and how in the movie you first meet him over the
phone and just hear his voice and how I thought
it was a recording of Burroughs himself. And he
went on about how great it is to work with Viggo
and how he insists on flying coach on airplanes and
always requests a compact car to pick up and drive
himself, and how the whole time they were filming
his scenes he never broke character even back at
the hotel, and that in the mornings the crew would
arrive at the location, and Viggo would already be
there on this own in costume, sitting in Burroughs'
chair reading Celine.

And I let him know how much I loved the Steve Buscemi scenes, which got huge laughs in both London and Toronto, and him driving the car really slowly then calling it "a perilous journey!" And Walter said, "Oh, I'm so glad you caught that. Yeah, that was fun," and he had a big smile on over those scenes.

And we also got personal. I got to thank him, actually twice, at length — how the Beat community is blessed that he was the man at the helm, that he was the guy to finally do this. And all the research he did, the complete emersion for eight years. That we couldn't have had a better man do it. And he was so grateful to hear this. And the whole time we're standing eye-to-eye, inches apart, not even blinking, but staring into the depths of each other's souls the way Neal and Allen do in the film and did in life.

And he went on about, "I feel like I know you after hearing about you all this time. It's so great to finally put a face to what I was thinking," as he leans back, holding up his hands and framing my face.

And he was so jazzed and thanked me, actually twice, for going to such lengths to see both versions — and how we could talk about the differences. And I could so honestly say how much better, more alive, faster tempoed, and more fun the new version is.

And we musta hugged in one way or another about 50 times during the night.

I still can't believe I've seen this movie *twice*, been to *two premieres on two continents*, and seen both the long *and* short versions! And it's still four months away from theaters!

8

On The Road
Comes Home —
The New York Premiere

The day of the *On The Road* premiere in New York
I was up at the NYPL trying to get through the
doors of the hermetically sealed vault of the Berg
Collection, home to a gazillion literary papers from
Emerson to Shelley — but most importantly the
entire Jack Kerouac collection! And when I say
"entire" I mean from grocery lists to manuscripts.
The book that lists his stuff there is single-spaced
and four inches thick! And of course the place is
harder to get into than the Oval Freakin Office, but
I figured with the mojo of this 12/12/12 opening I
oughta spin the tumblers and see what happens.

There's forms ya gotta fill out, cards ya gotta
get, background checks, *Jeopardy* questions, a
swimsuit competition — it's all way too much, but I
jump through every hoop and roll with every punch,
and they say they'll get back to me . . . in a week.

So, I go to the library's free computers to check

my email and find this from the film's director . . .

"Brian, Walter wanted to see if you would like to ride up with him to the premiere tonight."

! ! ! !

Done!

And then at the same time, I get an email from Teri McLuhan saying she can't join us as planned — so suddenly I've got an empty seat beside me for the premiere night adventure! But instantly, from the NYPL interwebs I'm able to track down The Mighty Debster, my intrepid partner from the MTV daze, the Emma Peel to my John Steed, a dynamic duo that got into every concert or mega-party we ever set our sights on.

"Does Walter want a pretty girl to join us in the car?" I email assistant Gerry.

Two minutes later: "Yes, one pretty girl in the car, please."

And BOOM weir on.

Back to the Jane Hotel to drop off the day and costume into night, and before I can get out the door there's an email telling me I've been approved to get into the Berg! I dunno how I dun it — and in 3 hours — but I'm sure it wasn't the swimsuit competition! So, I float out the door, and make my pilgrimage past John Lennon's house at 105 Bank Street, and although not a very religious type, I did a cross on my chest and say a little prayer of gratitude to John and The Spirits for lighting my Path.

Then cab it down to Walter's funky SoHo shelter from the storm, and there's the limo and there's the driver and before long, There's the birthday boy! And we're laughin and tellin stories, and I'm remembering my Spirit Guide role in this vital mission. As Gerry says, "It's your infectious enthusiasm." Everything positive, everything up, on our way to the New York premiere, the last in a looooong series for Che Walter on his North American crusade for truth, justice & the Road.

And of course Deb's not there yet, and he goes, "You don't promise a pretty girl and then not deliver. Just don't saying anything. But don't promise and not deliver," he's ribbin' me cuz we gotta get in the car and go, but just then, "There she is! Just a walkin' down the street singin' Do wah diddy, diddy-dum diddy-doo." And Boom weir off in the Starship, sittin' back that comfy way you can in limos, almost on beach chairs with your legs stretched out catching rays from the New York lights flashing in the windows like an old projector.

And Walter's holding these pages of a speech he's written, but he's not reading them, just looking down and saying, "I hope I don't forget anybody. Everybody's gonna be there tonight … oh man …" And I ask, "What about Steve Buscemi? Is he comin'?" And Walter's, "Oh my gawd, Buscemi!! Gerry, did we invite him?" And St. Gerry checks on his gizmo, and about a minute later reports he was invited but sent his regrets. And we're back to *Phoosh!* as we whoosh through the Sixth Avenue traffic. And I remind him the premiere is being held right around the corner from where Jack birthed the *On The Road* scroll, and Walter says, "There's no such thing as coincidences," and twinkles through the flashing night lights.

And as we turn onto the block we can see the mobs on the sidewalks and the whole scene, and the driver starts to slow down right in front of the red carpet and Walter calls out, "No, no, drive up ahead, don't let me out here!!" not wanting to step into the flashbulb blitzkrieg. We get our shit together in the darkness of the stretch-Hudson, and then it's, "Go!" and we open the door and stride as quickly as we can into the theater, people calling, "Walter!" from all directions, and he grabs Deb on one side and me on the other and we were pretending like we were in the middle of some great conversation for the distance between the car and the glass theater doors. Funny, fast, and efficient.

And there's the girls with the clipboards, and the seas part and we sail into the safe harbor of the lobby. Outside were the unaccredited paparazzi. Inside there's a whole Special Forces unit of them — and this time there's no getting around it. But we slip behind the photographer's backdrop for a deep breath and a twinkling jazzed regrouping before facing that first line of cameras both still and rolling, then a whole wall lined with reporters with notebooks and recorders and accreditation around their necks. While hanging backstage I spot the crew's cheat-sheets — pages with color photos of each of the expected celebs so the door crew know the faces when they appear. Good look-out.

Turns out all the seats in the theater are assigned, so you don't just get a ticket, you get a specific seat like at a concert. Once Debs and I score our juicy pair, we go pre-scout the venue and sure enough we're in primetime dead-center, and I see some cat near-about our seats, and ask how he came to be here, thinkin this whole row will be friends n family, and he said, "I'm a friend of one of the actors." "Oh, nice. Which one?" And he says, "Garrett." And I'm like, "Oh great!" And he asks about me, and I start tellin' him, and he's like, "I've heard of you! You wrote those great pieces. Yeah, Garrett was telling me about you." And I'm thinkin', this is going well so far.

So, Deb & I prankster about for a bit, checkin' the scene, eavesdropping on anticipatory conversations, looking into the faces of all the beautiful people who are about to go On The Road. And there's this guy who looks like Michael Stipe who sang at the Hurricane Sandy benefit last night at Madison Square Garden, but I'm thinkin, "Na, that's just somebody who looks like him." And I take a roll down the aisles proudly wearing my American flag shirt that later gets raved about at the afterparty for happily waving it in this second term engagement season, and I'm lookin for familiar Beat faces but this is the film bidniss and not exactly St.-Mark's-On-The-Bowery.

Then finally we all take our seats and I'm makin' friends in about four different directions, including with these crazy red-haired girls who keep droppin booze bottles on the clanking floor all night which was really funny and very *On The Road* but I bet some less-than-spirited patrons may have been offended at their lack of decorum at this serious occasion — but to me they were just quiet Jacks laughing in the immensity of it.

And soon some IFC honcho comes on stage and praises Walter up down and sideways as "a master filmmaker and one of the best cinematic storytellers in the world," then Walter comes out and he's all, "Geez, well now I'm really trembling a little after that introduction!"

Then goes, "And I'm also nervous to be here because *On The Road* was birthed (*he's using my word!!*) just three blocks from here," And I'm, "No way! He's doin' my bit! He remembered!! Cool!" And then he says, "It was written on 20th Street and 9th Avenue in April 1951, and I want to thank my good friend Brian Hassett, who is here tonight,

for reminding me." And I'm, *No way!!* Not only
does he thank me, but I'm the first person he
mentions in his New York premiere night speech!!
What the?!?!

Then he goes on and talks about the movie
and thanks the IFC people and John Sampas and
Ann Charters and others but I barely heard it cuz I
was still in such a tizzy over him thanking me!! . .
. First!! And then he does it again! Crazy! Pinch
me!

Then Walter goes on all these incredible off-the-
cuff riffs covering any number of subjects. Like, "I
had a passion for the book that was triggered when
I first read it in 1974 when I was entering university
in Brazil which was living through the dark ages
of a military dictatorship, and the book carried
all the freedoms we were seeking but not able to
experience, so it had a very resonant quality. But I
knew that that wasn't enough of a reason to begin
an adaptation, so I proposed to American Zoetrope
to do a documentary in search of a possible film
based on *On The Road*. And they went for this
insane idea! And for six years we crisscrossed
America on the paths Kerouac had taken when
he wrote *On The Road*, and we met with the
characters of the book who are still alive and they
were extremely generous to us. We talked to the
poets of that generation that changed the cultural
landscape not only of this country but of Brazil as
well. Lawrence Ferlinghetti, Michael McClure, Diane
DiPrima, Amiri Baraka, Hettie Jones — it was a
unique experience because I had never met younger
70-year-olds than this group, because they had kept
two things intact — their beliefs and their integrity.
And that's very very hard to keep in the long run."

And then he brings out the actors in this cool
way — in the order in which they first committed
to the film. First it's Kirsten Dunst who plays the
person he met on the project who most impressed
him — Carolyn Cassady. "In meeting Carolyn in

2005, I was so impacted by the intelligence and the sensitivity of that unique woman, and I thought that only an actress with those qualities could play her. Please welcome Kirsten Dunst."

Then he goes into this whole story about a friend of his who saw an advance screening of *Into The Wild* and immediately called Walter about the perfect actress to play Marylou, and he wrote the unknown's name down on a napkin: "Kristen Stewart" "And when I first met her in 2007 she had such an in-depth understanding of what *On The Road* was about and knew the book inside out, and she was 17."

Then ... "When Garrett Hedlund drove from Northern Minnesota for three days to the audition in Los Angeles, he brought such electricity and life to Dean that we knew we had found one of the most difficult characters to cast, and that electricity never dissipated — but what I didn't know is that he would be such a great Road companion."

And then he intros Sam Riley with, "One day I saw *Control*, and for those of you who love cinema, you know how impactful that could be. Seeing Sam Riley in that film was something I wasn't going to forget. There was such intelligence in the performance, such intensity, but also in the non-verbal there was the capacity to understand and decode the world. And these are qualities writers have, and that we wanted to have to bring Sal to the world."

Then he says, "I have to confess I belong to a specific religion that states — there is no independent film without Steve Buscemi." Gets a big laugh. "Many thanks to him for helping, not only for being in the film but for recommending so many great actors that we ended up casting in it. You're wonderful."

And then the movie happens — my *fifth* time seeing it on the big screen (!) and it hasn't even opened yet — and I kinda lost it at the Orgone

Accumulator scene. Now that I know it's coming, I see Viggo as Bill as so freakin' funny in this scene, it's just nuts in the Crazy Dept., and before he ever climbs into that outhouse I'm laughing my head off and infect the rows around me so by the time he finally sticks his head in the window our whole section is roaring.

Then the movie's over to many whoops and whistles and raucous applause, and it's one of my favorite times on earth — being in a movie theater right after *On The Road* ends, and eavesdropping on conversations and talking to people and looking into their movie screen faces for the story they tell, and of course every face is aglow and the room's a Marshall stack of fast talking New Yorkers all soloing at once, but you can pick out fragments "... the cinematography ... ," "... that guy who played Ginsberg ... ," "... those party scenes were great!" "... and when he starts to cry at the end ..."

And after much beaming Debs and I finally weave out front and hang under the marquee and I ask this group of models what they thought (purely research, you understand) and the prettiest one goes, "AMAZING!" unabashedly beaming, almost giggling in joy.

And we schmooze our way around the circle until the afterglow begins to fade, and it's like, "Okay, let's hit the party." But of course there's no cabs at the moment you need one, so we mosey on down to 9th Avenue yakin our fool heads off ... What about Kristen Stewart?! and How about that soundtrack?! And Debs is goin' on about the costumes and how the people look and how they totally brought post-war America to life.

And we get to the and of course there's no cabs there either, and by now a whole krewe from outside the movie including the models have caught up with us, and we'd need about 3 cabs anyway, and Deb goes, "It's really close, let's just start walkin," and of course — Bing Bing Bing — "And if we don't get one by 20th Street, wheel swing past ol' Jack's house on the way to the party!"

Then on the very first corner there's this deli and I'm like, "My God! *I'm in New York!*" And dash in for a cold Heineken Road jar … because I can. And now weir really rollin and I *know* no fleet of cabs are comin so I start tellin' the gang the whole story of the 50th Anniversary of Jack writing *On The Road* show I produced — which started by going to this house on 20th Street and then walking to the corner to find the closest bar and talking them into giving me the place for the night Jack started writing The Scroll. And one of the krewe actually LIVES on this block of 20th and didn't know this was The Street!

And just as the tour bus is approaching the sacred site, I see someone go up the stoop and through the front door! I scootch up ahead and somehow get the guy's attention, and he's squintin through two sets of doors at this maniac at his gate, then I start waving him out and gosh darn if he doesn't come!

"Hey man! You know who used to live here?"

"I sure do," the shy guys says.

"Well, we were just at the premiere of his movie! Of the book that was written right here in this apartment!"

"You're kidding?! The premiere was tonight?!"

"Yeah, it's great, you're gonna love it. Hey — what apartment are you in?"

He points up to the second floor, "Right here in number 2."

And I fairly yell, "*THAT WAS JACK'S APARTMENT!!!*"

And he goes, "Yeah, I know," and smiles a twinkle.

I figured he didn't want to have our whole krewe up to his place without any warning, so we just blessed him, and thanked him, and buzzed him, and left him with a big glow as we continued our flow to the aftershow.

And Aretha's flyin through my head — *"This is the house that Jack built, y'all, remember this house ..."*

"I stopped at John's place on the way to the premiere, and Jack's house after the premiere!" I'm gushing like a geyser and dancing down the street like a dingledodie delirious with everything at the same time and spinning like a centerlight top, and everybody goes, *"Awwww ... that Brian guy's nuts!"*

Then we get to the corner of the party, and now *Deb* starts jumping up and down! "Oh my God, *it's at The Top of The Standard?!?!"* and starts screamin and laughin and yankin on my arm like a little kid about to go on her favorite ride!

Everything had already taken on that surreal tone of a night in magic places in endless New York ... and we hadn't even gotten to the playground in the sky yet!

And just as a last throw-ya-off and freak-ya-out before you step into Netherland, the elevators have these crazy mirrors, and trippy lights, and the girls

110

are gorgeous, and the guys are crackin jokes, and we're travelin straight up at the speed of light.

And — BOOM — into the Gilded Age, in a place that looks for all the world like Windows On The World at the top of the World Trade Center — a high-rise along the Hudson with _no_ buildings out the windows — because it's in the West Village you can just see forever out the vertical frames of floor-to-ceiling glass. And there's Walter being the gracious host, greeting everyone at the door as they arrive, and I tell him about the pilgrimage to Jack's house and meeting the current resident, and he's shaking his head, "Only you, amigo!" And another big hug and cheek kiss and wild night with the mad ones was just beginning.

Then he leans in and tells me Patti Smith was at the movie, but he doesn't know if she's here at the party or not.

And I'm like, "Got it." Boom: Mission Patti. Find her in about 3 secs. Back to Walter. "She's right there by the window," I nod. He smiles. "Anybody else you want me to find?" We laugh, and I'm off to the party.

And right away his saintly assistant Gerry goes, "Oh, there's something Walter asked me to give you," and pulls out these magic beans — tiny _On The Road_ buttons based on the orange-covered first edition I ever owned!

And I wander a few more feet and there's ol' John Sampas ... and we're all super friendly. I know bad shit's gone down, but he was really helpful to Walter and the film, and I thanked him for that, and he was all wide smiles and really liked how the movie turned out.

And there's Hal Willner the forever music supervisor of _Saturday Night Live_ and movies like _Howl_ and _Gonzo_ and also produced a bunch of Allen and Burroughs' albums, and posthumous Lenny Bruce and Edgar Allen Poe, and so he's right in with the family of crazee Roadsters, and we jammed on

111

the fragments of lost memories in the mindfield landscape.

And then there's Ann Charters and Regina Weinreich at a nice corner table overlookin the city, and just like in the movie — the women are most prevalent.

And after scouting the room, I realize the headliners' section was the sunken booth area by the front door, and as I head down into it I overhear the undercover security protecting the stars saying, "He's okay, I saw him with Walter," and Boom — I'm in. And there's Garrett beaming, and we finally talk, and he knows who I am, but he's still in official promo mode, all polite and by-the-books, but a while later I spin back and he's got a pack of cigs in his hand. "You goin' up for a smoke?" The eyebrow high-five, and weir off.

The Roof! I'm Home! They have a whole closed-in heated plastic room up there, but the real scene is the wide open spaces — most of the entire roof is a giant party space with views in every direction around this port city, and weir just blazing as the night starts kickin' in, and Kirsten joins us, and some director doing Garrett's next movie, and Debs is there refraining Amsterdam, and we're finally havin' a yak about all things Beat, and Garrett tells me the two scenes he had to audition for the role were the suicide rap and the 4-way sex letter. I guess Walter felt if you could deliver those two solos you could be in the band. And I flashed back to Walter saying how he loved Garrett's acting but didn't know then what a great road buddy he'd turn out to be.

Then after a smoke or three we start headin' back down the stairwell to the party, but up comes brother Ben and Katia, Garrett's friend couple from our row at the premiere, and suddenly weir having this reunion on the landing of a stairwell with a glass wall behind us facing uptown New York City, and a party ensues, and then Boom, Sam Riley appears at the top of the stairs, and Garrett goes into an incredible Sam impersonation, and MAN has this guy got the gift for it!! He does Riley better than Riley. And suddenly Jack and Neal are together again hangin' in the stairwell, riffin off each other 50 years later. And THEN Kristen Stewart comes walkin down the stairs, and suddenly it's the whole Road crew! hanging on a stairwell balcony, only missing Big Al Hinkle, who we could see on the street below running out for more rolling papers, as weir looking over twinkling New York with Neal carrying on multiple conversations in multiple voices at once.

And then back to the party and Walter introduces me to Kristen Stewart, which is such a strange and unexpected thing that he has to be dealing with with this movie. Like, nobody in it was supposed to be a movie star. The leads were all cast because they were unidentifiable fresh faces — film goers were already coming in with such fixed images in their minds as to what the characters looked like, the filmmakers couldn't also have actors with established characters affixed. So they cast all relative unknowns in the main roles. Then lo and behold, Kristen Stewart becomes the biggest grossing actress of 2012 before the movie even comes out! So Walter, and her, and everyone, have to deal with this.

But I get to hang with the mega-star for a while, and man, she's so petite you could put her in your pocket! And she's bookish, and reserved, and 180 degrees different than Marylou. We talk about indie film, and she confirms my assumption that's she's gonna do them the rest of her life. We didn't say it, but this is a 22-year-old indie chick who fluked into the biggest movie franchise of the last few years and she never has to work another day in her life. Yet she is going to be so many different interesting characters in the years to come. I tell her the truth — that she brought Marylou more to life than Jack did, but she would hear none of it. To her, it was all Jack. And I beamed.

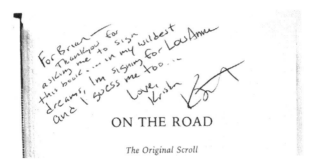

ON THE ROAD

The Original Scroll

Then back to the center bar with windows out three sides, and now it's lookin' like The Rainbow Room, and all New York is spinning, and there's the krewe from the Jack's house walk! And we start riffin', and I pull out my Scroll book, and they start jammin and reading passages from it, and then 20th Street homie sez, "You got a favorite part?" and hands me back The Bible and I play some boppin' "Hearing Shearing" in the bull's-eye center of the room, Jack's voice in the house, and the whole krewe whoopin' and the Gold Club bartenders bug-eyed, and the neighbors nodding, as the bass player hunched over and thrummed the beat, faster and faster it seemed! And oh, Mighty Jack — his songs still singin' and swingin' above old New York ...

114

And suddenly there's Walter! And we hug and he says he has to go find somebody and I'm "Okay," and we wander off on some mission. I dunno what we were doin' but we ended up on the roof and back again and I dunno if we ever accomplished anything but I told him, "Your kids are all gathered in the corner — you should go see them." And this was the most amazing thing — in this beautiful penthouse skyline scene where I would not and did not take any pictures except for the one I'll share shortly, but in the corner of this mobbed premiere party, Garrett, Kirsten, Kristen, and Sam were able to sit side-by-side in this alcove by the window, the four of them together again for perhaps the first time since they were all crammed in a '49 Hudson for months, and able to enjoy the reunion together. And it's so obvious how close they all are — it was like my high school reunion a couple years ago — talkin', laughin' and huggin' all at the same time.

And like a high school reunion, things started to get crazy, people were making out, people were disappearing, people were reappearing, and all of sudden I'm talking to Michael Stipe, and he's a leprechaun, and I ask him how it felt to be out on stage at MSG last night for the first time in years, and he kind of avoids the question, then I ask him again, and he says he hadn't planned to do it, and then I asked him again how it felt to be out there on that stage, and he looked away. Then he smiled a beam and looked back and twinkled, "It felt good."

And then Patti Smith comes by and we chat for a bit about the old St. Mark's Church scene, and she says it's still happening, and then Walter shows up and we form a trio, and I'm like, "Wait a minute," and I pull out the camera and capture these two artists gushing over the others' work.

And they had a great long one-on-one, and she called the movie "authentic" and that's the kind of thing you want to hear from someone who knows the meaning of that word.

And then there was the part about … I hated that I was comped and on-the-list for this whole thing. There wasn't a single sneaking in Prankster prank involved anywhere and I hadn't really broken a serious rule all night as far as I could tell.

But then the party was suddenly over, and all these strange people were streaming into the club who weren't at the event … and ol' fast-thinking Deb, Master Of All Things, gets us to boost a booth from the sunken celeb scene, then scores a bucket of fresh ice from one table, and a bottle of juice mixer from another, then I dump out a glass full of stir-sticks for a clean one, and she does the same from the next table, and before long we've got a booth and a stocked private bar overlookin Manhattan with a nearly full bottle of Grey Goose Vodka that Deb says would be $400 to be sitting here with.

116

And the staff comes and cleans up the other booths all around us to a pristine club-opening state, but our scene looked like New Year's Eve at 3AM, with two happy semi-sober streamer-covered revelers still poundin them back.

And from this well-stocked cockpit, the last Beats holding the fort saw out the night, overlooking the twinkling Christmas of lower Manhattan, curved booths at our back, an open bar at our knees, and more stories to tell than we could ever get through.

9

Woodstock
with The Pranksters

First published on BrianHassett.com shortly after it happened — August 2014.

"I've got to get back to the land and set my soul free ..."

Two of the coolest events of the '60s just came together in the 21st century — and I lived it from start to finish.

The Merry Pranksters' Bus, the original of which pulled out of Ken Kesey's house in La Honda on my June 14th birthday in 1964, came to Max Yasgur's farm where Woodstock was born in 1969. Since then, each of these events — painted buses traveling around full of fun-loving friends, and gatherings in fields for weekend concert communes — have become part of world-wide culture.

But this is where it all began — with a Bang!

And this time it all began with an unplanned dash — when the 2014 50th anniversary Kesey krewe got cancelled last minute out of some other festival and suddenly was heading for ... Woodstock! ... of course! ... where it was supposed to be goin' in the first damn place!

Mmmm ... home again ... Gotta be *there* — on Max's farm, where Woodstock as we know it began ... where the Oregon creamery boys first joined up with the New York dairy farmer.

If you don't know the backstory on Max — he was a respected, if iconoclastic, "elder statesman" farmer and thousand-acre landowner in this area of Sullivan County, NY, even though he was only 49 years old at the time of the festival. (And what a 50th he must have had that December!) Max was known to speak his mind and go his own way in a conservative old-world rural culture that was very much go-along-get-along.

The festival organizers were kicked off of their months-in-development site just 30 days before the festival was to begin. Max had been reading in the local papers about the trouble "these kids" were having, and told them when they first met, "I want to help you boys. You got the raw end of the deal." He had a very evolved philosophy of equality and justice — a living 20th century Thoreau, he was a pro-active ethicist for whom a handshake was a binding contract — and injustice did not sit well with him.

Plus, he was also a pretty sharp businessman. Picture Woody Allen meets Jack Benny — as Max is noodling around his farm all Woodstock weekend licking the end of his pencil and jotting down every bucket of milk a cow didn't deliver to make sure he was covered for it. But beyond his pencilings, because it was Max, and the respectful relationship they evolved, the promoters spent months and tens of thousands of extra dollars restoring his land to what it was when they arrived.

One story, to give you the idea, and something only his wife Miriam could relate: When word spread that Max was talking to these "hippies" about having this banned festival on his farm, somebody put up a sign along the Route 17B road in front of his house — "Stop Max's hippy music festival — Buy no milk." When Max & Miriam saw it for the first time, as she recalled — "I thought, 'You don't know Max. Now it's going to happen.' That did it. He just turned to me and said, 'Is it alright with you?' ... I knew he was not going to get past this sign, so I said, 'I guess we're gonna have a festival.' And he said, 'Yup, we're gonna have a festival.' And that was it."

Max would have been a great political leader or writer or millionaire businessman if just a couple cells had been different. But ol' Jack Fate cast this activist philosopher as a farmer — who happened to have a perfect natural amphitheater in the same neck of the world as that little artists' colony that Dylan happened to stumble into a few summers earlier.

And thus, in one of the festival's innumerable karmic twists, the organizers were thrown out of the town of Wallkill and onto Max Yasgur's farm along Happy Avenue in Bethel(hem). There was a whole lotta Shinin' goin' on with this man and this moment.

And up to his homestead we did roll — bought in 1985 by Roy Howard and now run by his widow, Jeryl Abramson, in The Spirit, letting Woodstockians the whirled over gather on Max's land every anniversary since 1998. And this was only the second year it's been legal!

As soon as you come up the small rise onto the land — there's Max's house — where the deal for the festival was consummated — and where it's honored with an

official historical marker befitting an official historic
figure.

And then there it is ... The Bus! The Magic Bus.
The Kesey Bus. Furthur. The psychedelic painted
school bus that spawned it all.
It wasn't the same Beat-up 1939 International
Harvester that Neal Cassady drove across the country
in 1964 ad came to Woodstock in '69, but as Father Ken
maintained: It was the same spirit — much like Max's
homestead wasn't the actual field for the concert in 1969
— but was the same spirit being created by its current
inhabitants.
In the Crazy Karma 2014 Dept.: So, we hang out
Thursday night in the anticipation glow, then I retired
to the nearby cheap motor hotel I found for the night
— flipped on the CNN — and there's Kesey's Bus!! .
. . wait–*what?!?!* And there's Kesey & Babbs talkin'
about La Honda and the birth of it all! And they're
ravin' on about Kerouac!!! Rub my eyes and ding my
bell! It's CNN's series *The Sixties,* and the "*Sex, Drugs,
& Rock n Roll*" episode! Jack didn't make Woodstock or
ride on The Bus — but here he was being described on
CNN as The Father of us all ! — the On The Road back-
to-the-land mountain climbing searcher who put into

poetic prose the rose we were all smelling so sweetly.

And as this photo shows — the Chief saw to it that they were reunited in the driver's cockpit of the new starship to deep space.

On Friday morning, there was Zane bright and early manning the merch tent, selling everything from painted toy buses and fridge magnets to Prankster t-shirts and DVDs of "the world's mightiest home movie" as the original Pranksters dubbed their footage from the first cross-country trip.

Floating around The Bus were the film crew — appropriately from British Columbia — and all sorts of Next Generation Pranksters like Chris Foster who appeared as The Wizard, Carmen Miranda, and a psychedelic cowboy over each of the three days, and actually lives in Bloomington, Indiana, where I'd just recently summited with Neal's son John Cassady, director Walter Salles, and the *Road* scroll preserver Jim Canary for the *On The Road* movie premiere.

But this was no dosed-kool-aid acid party. It was a business, as they're rightfully concerned The Bus is a blazing target in this crazy militarized America — so they have to play it clean.

The real action and Spirit evocation was out in the woods where decades of the owners hosting events had resulted in dirt roads and footpaths and campsites and drum circle centers and full-on stages for non-stop performances all day and night. There were deliciously elaborate kitchens making the best pizza I've had since New York, and a breakfast guy making vegi-rich omelets that put the best restaurants to shame — in price and quality. Then there was the giant tent general store selling everything — camping supplies, toiletries, first-aid stuff, cigs, batteries and whatever a prankster or camper of eternity might need.

Then there were the art installations, like Christopher VanderEssen's, who created a florescent blacklight dreamcatcher weaving through the woods.

It's where you'd meet people named Dragon Fly or Morning Glory, and every person is saying "High" to every other person in this church of camaraderie. . . . "Everywhere was a song and a celebration ..."

Meanwhile, back at The Bus, I ended up talking to this colorful couple, Rick and Sherry. He went to the first Woodstock, arriving Thursday morning, parking his car on site, settin up their tent in the woods, then wandering over to the field where they found a spot 30 feet from the stage and never moved (or went back to their tent and car) until Monday! He was wearing this cap of rainbow dreads, and she was under a colorful jester's hat with dangling bells, and to be quite confessional, I was feeling a little under-dressed.

And they were like most of the people I met here — super smart. This wasn't a bunch of brain-dead loogans, but rather highly evolved explorers and sophisticated pranksters. People who knew how to Adventure, and survive on a farm for a long weekend, and how to make fun happen. In fact, it was over an in-depth discussion of Obamacare (not positive) that Rick & Sherry & I really bonded, and were joined by The Wizard of Wonder, Chris Foster, talking through his costume, and the four of us thereafter became a fairly inseparable

quartet — and by Sunday knew we would be for life.

The Spirit of Woodstock was alive — and being created by the people — not rock stars or anyone else dictating from on high. It was an organic connection among souls who'd been driven to drive some distance to spend a formless whacky weekend in the woods. Not only was no one aggressively drunk, but I never heard a harsh word spoken over four days. When I first heard someone impatient and frustrated in "the real world" a few days later, it sounded so foreign and out of place and unnecessary and unhappy.

And that's what these things do — the fabric of your soul becomes dipped in a rainbow dye and permanently transformed by the swirling colors of love and happiness and peacefulness and camaraderie all collectively blending together — all based on happenstance ... with a purpose. Who knows what's going to happen or who you're going to meet? But tossing yourself into this tribal gathering of like-minded Adventurers, you'll go lots of somewheres cool. Like the endless jam sessions going on all over the fields — with the Grateful Dead dominating the airwaves.

Then there was the woman running the booth for the non-profit Eden's Rose Foundation that sells handmade alpaca clothes and hardwood carvings (including of the Ice Cream Kid and Cats Under The Stars and all sorts of Grateful Dead images) made

by native tribes in the jungles of Peru and Brazil and
Bolivia, and the money goes directly back to the local
tribes to keep their ancient cultures self-sustaining.

And hanging here at this soulful booth I learned
about "spunions" — the new term for people who are
well spun and happily blazing in the middle of the
night. And in this scene — where *no one* is drunk and
stumbling around and starting fights, but so many
are so high — it really puts a lie to our drug & alcohol
laws. High people wander through the woods like a
pack of wild comedians cracking each other up, their
laughter heard long before you see them, or like gentle
little children in a fairy tale amazed at everything they
see. Hanging at the booth and seeing all the traffic flow
in and out, it would have been completely different if
they were as drunk as they were high.

There was this HUGE arc of people — an
anthropologists delight! — from 4 & 5 year old kids
running around playing, to 70 & 80 year olds shuffling
along who'd been at the first Woodstock — and
both ends of the spectrum beaming beatific faces of
joy. Whatever your age, there was a gorgeous farmful of
friendly people to play with.

And a funny-nice thing from Sunday afternoon
— all weekend we'd been hearing excellent bands play
their own stuff along with The Dead, The Band, Santana,
CSNY, etc. ... as you do at any of these Woodstock
reunions or music festivals in the woods. But all of a
sudden I'm hearing some girl singing *Brand New Key*
by Melanie!

"No way! This is so great!" Melanie and I had a
memorable flirty evening on the night of the Folk City
Anniversary Concert and afterparty in New York in
1980-something, and I always thought she was the
real deal — very spiritual and spirited. So, I'm boppin'
away to this, and what does the girl singer on stage do
next? but the hit song Melanie wrote about her historic

126

unplanned performance at Woodstock, *Candles In The Rain.*

And dancing in front of the stage is Rachel, who'd been Stage Manager on the main double-stage *all weekend.* You don't meet many women stage managers period, let alone running the main stage of a major festival — with acts one after another using two stages side-by-side so each band has the other's performance time to set up. And they had a different act every 15, 30, 45 minutes from 9:30AM till 3AM. Finally by Sunday afternoon here she was dancing with me and everybody else to *Candles In The Rain.* And after it's over we have a big hug, and I say, "How great is it to hear Melanie played at Woodstock?!"

And she goes, "And by her daughter no less!"
"*What?!?!*"

And sure enough ... a little later I'm hangin' at the Blue Bomber which was centrally located between The Bus and The Woods, and I look over next to me and there she is! Jeordie, Melanie's daughter, with her guitar player! And the poor bastards are trying to open some nice indi beers without an opener. See ... that's the difference between our two countries — even cool Americans don't know how to pop a cold one with a lighter. And these micro-breweries have quite the pop with their lively brews — and I could send those puppies half-way across the field, impressing the hell out of ol' Melanie Jr. And suddenly we're huggin' n flirtin' and I'm thinkin' this whole Woodstock thing is alright.

Back at The Bus, there were any number of adventures. At one point they said they wanted to go "out front" to take some pictures with The Bus on The Farm. 'Course I wanted to be in on that, but Prankster plans are like dreams — they might be real or they might go poof — they might be right now, or in ten days, or just a goof.

At some point I'm hanging in the woods at the dual main stages when a telepathic spark went off in me bean — "Wait a minute — maybe they're takin' the picture!" And as I walked out into the clearing — sure enough — The Bus was missing! I scooched as fast as my skinny legs could scooch me back to The Mighty Blue Bomber, jumped in to go find The Bus, and Boom! right around the corner there they were parked under Yasgur's big barn sign! Bolted over with my camera ... just as they were coming down off the roof! . . . Bummer!!

But there was no way I was going to miss this if I could do anything about it, so I ran over and spotted this girl Angie Lee I'd been talking to in the scene, handed her my camera with instructions to shoot away like crazy, then ran to the back of the bus before everyone got off, and climbed on up and said I *had* to get my pic with the Woodstock and Yasgur's signs — which was a bit forward of me telling these stray cat Pranksters what to do — but sure enough they went for it — and it led to a whole new round of shots — with other photographers falling into the scene who'd missed the spontaneous moment earlier now catching it, and suddenly there was

a whole second photoshoot going down cuz I insisted on it!

As my new best friend Sherry wisely says, "What's meant to be will not pass you by."

See ... these are the truths you re-learn at Woodstock.

Or there was the time The Bus was thinking of maybe going to the original Woodstock site and museum just a mile down Route 17B at the new Bethel Woods Arts Center. 'Course this plan muddled around all day until I decided I wanted to go over there for reasons also including porcelain facilities and free wifi. So I did, parking with a nice view of the road, and sure enough before long this bright blue bus came barreling along out of the dark tree tunnel with a loaded rooftop including Thumpah tootling the multitudes with his flute and everyone whooping and waving and pranking the unsuspecting touri wandering the fancy grounds.

And just as this was happening, in the magic Crazy Karma synch that *is* Pranksterhood, Museum Director Wade was just leaving for the day and spotted them and screeched over in his car, and offered to let The Bus drive up the walkway to the front doors of the museum! So, suddenly there was the larger-than-life psychedelic Magic Bus parked at the doors to Woodstock, just like the first Bus had been. And of course Mr. Museum Director comps us all in (normally $15 per) and before you know it the unsuspecting museum goers are overrun with Camp Prankster colors and voices and giggles and music.

I hadn't yet shown Zane the fancy Bethel Woods pamphlet that had an aerial shot of the '69 crowd on the front cover — *and a Prankster bus on the back!*

And just as I'm showing him this, we turn a corner in the museum — and there it is! A bus based on his Dad's is the promotional and literal centerpiece of

The Woodstock Museum! And we climb aboard and
... they've made a movie about The Bus and the Hog
Farm that's playing on the inside windshield of the
bus! And they're interviewing Max's son Sam ... and I'm
... sitting with Ken's son Zane ... in a psychedelic school
bus at Woodstock watching a movie about his Dad's
psychedelic school bus at Woodstock ... while Furthur's
sitting out front!

Mind = blown!

Or there was the time we all went for a Pranksters
Walkabout late Saturday night, about 20 of us in a
roaming nomadic crazy loud krewe with light sticks
and magic wands and guitars and flutes and drums and
pretty girls and silly boys making noise and begetting
smiles and breaking into song as we ambled along.

At some point we found ourselves at the giant
nearly abandoned 3-ring drum circle in the jungle dark,
and the band members and some singers broke into
funny falsetto versions of Led Zeppelin songs, while
Zane's throwing out zany one-liners like his father
would — delivered dry and coming from some alternate
universe. Somebody mentioned the bell that fell off the
bus and almost hit the follow car, and he goes, "That
car isn't done being hit yet." Somebody said, "There's
certain things that must remain unsaid." Zane pops,
"That's the first rule of Prankster Club."

And it was all in perfect harmony with The
Unspoken Thing — San Francisco comic and de facto
Prankster Robin Williams ... who we just lost and were
collectively mourning.

It wasn't dark, but it was getting there. Comedy
in the dark, but not dark comedy. You didn't know
who was riffing unless you recognized their voice, and
everyone was playing along, banging the gong, beating
the drum, all with a Robert Plant falsetto as the giggling
soundtrack.

Or there was that sunset moment on Sunday where

130

I was tuned into the simultaneous sacredness of the celestial and human event, and going around suggesting to people like new Prankster Moray that I use their camera to take pics of them in that special sunset light, when Zane picked up on what I was doing, the moment I was capturing, and he rounded up the stray cat krewe and wandered us out to the open field between Max's house and barn and took our jumping-for-joy-Woodstock photos.

And Zane tells us this story of how his Dad would gather people for sunset and watch for the green flash of light just as the sun crosses out of sight, and of course we all do this ... and I think I'm seeing flashes — but it may have been from all the jumping we just did!

Anyway, as he's telling the story in his big booming Oregon farmer Kesey voice — he was looking me right in the eye and telling it directly to me. And I'm thinkin' this whole Prankster thing is alright.

Later I started riffing with the Canadian film crew, some B.C. buds that went by Colby and Puds, and even though it's late in the proceedings I'm spewing my usual nonsense that to some people occasionally sounds articulate, and Puds sez, "I gotta interview you for the movie. Would you mind?" It felt like I hadn't had a shower since July or a night's sleep since June, but The Bus was clanging it's bell to leave for D.C. in the morning, and now the bell hath tolled for thee.

Puds starts lookin around for a set — someone's on The Bus doin' sumpthin' — and he remembers the giant Woodstock banner he bought that afternoon using Prankster dollars, which was just play money they printed but were able to trade for cool shit. So, BOOM! We hang the flag over the inside of the back door of their equipment truck (which Zane calls, "our trunk") and climb inside and do a whole long interview there where I riffed on some lessons I learned from Father Ken (out first hang tales now available in my book *The Hitchhiker's Guide to Jack Kerouac*), and how I could see the father in the son with his quick dry one-liners, and how the bus has influenced generations.

Even in my three-days-of-Woodstock madness, I knew any answer had to be 15 or 30 seconds tops. No long winding Brian stories here — conscious to speak in soundbites cuz they're making such an epic new Mightiest Home Movie that there's gonna be a whole lotta noodles to tootle. And sure enough I pulled it off and made the final cut and am in their Bus Trip movie *Going Furthur*.

And by the time we're done, it was 10:30 Sunday night, and Lieutenant Hassett's watchin' his watch and knows the only nearby beer store is closing at 11, so in this wonderful living flashback to our Canadian roots, me and ol' B.C. Puds make a last-dash Beer Run just like the old days — two wise Canucks swimming away from the ducks to try our luck and sure enough! Bingo! We're bongo with bounties of brewskies for blast-off!

And after Zane and I had not really connected when I first arrived, by the end of the last day, it was just he and I together at the back of The Bus as he wound up the giant flags into ropes so he could tie them to the ship — the Stars & Stripes and the Oregon State (the only

132

state flag in America with something on both sides, he
tells me with pride) in preparation for their highway-
driving departure in the morning. It was just the two
of us rapping and wrapping the show — about what
worked (everything above plus the impromptu gig they
did one morning that I missed), and what didn't (they
shoulda been parked down in the woods), but he had a
beatific smiling calm about him that another show was
successfully done, and of all the sites they visited this
was the first one The Bus had been to before, and that
living history was meeting living history (maybe it was
me who said that) and that the two family reunions had
blended so well.

And by now the Woodstockians and Pranksters have
morphed back into the world, and maybe you can't even
recognize who we are. And The Bus has continued it's
Trip, tootling the multitudes in Washington and New
York and Cleveland and Chicago on the never-ending
Road Trip started by Jack and driven by Neal and
jumped on by Jerry and captained by Ken that's still
hugging hearts with loving arms and ever going . . .

10

Pranksters in Wonderland

Somewhere in America . . .
Pranksters are gathering . . .
And in this case it was Wonderland.

A dozen acres of wilderness hills and valleys, with a
sunken natural amphitheater on the highest point of
land in sight.

150 or so Pranksters came from across the land,
traveling by every mode there is, to play the play like
only Pranksters play. No passengers. Everyone here's a
participant, a character — a bunch of characters.

There were babies, under 10s, tweens, teenagers,
20-somethings and every-somethings through their
70s ... everyone interacting on an equal level ... no
cliques ... no divisions ... no separation ... and everyone
in a beaming mood all weekend ... nuthin' but fun on
so many levels in SO many locations — the house, the

front porch, the covered shed, the clothes painting area, the RVs, the Bertha Bus scene, the sign painting scene, the yurt, the first party tent, the second party tent, the Mad Hatter hat, the 300 section looking down on the amphitheater, the natural balcony level, the stage pit, the bonfire pit, the camping scene, the field-size chess table and other installations — that's about *17* wink wink different scenes right off the top ...

And then there's the part where right afterwards people were saying things like . . .

"One week ago, I left New York to see people I've never met and to experience something like I have never experienced before. It was by far the most memorable weekend of my entire life, and I cannot express enough my love for each person I met. You all radiated an energy that I can't even put into words. And you brought the spirits that couldn't be there right to the party. Sometimes you invite spirits and they don't show, but with this amount of positive energy and love in the air, the spirits couldn't help but be there with us!"

Or . . .

"One day at your party was better than my entire
vacation in Hawaii last week. It's one thing to be in
paradise, but quite another to be around incredible
people. I just lost two of my mentors in the space of
a few days and I was feeling pretty down about it all
... and suddenly there I am standing in front of the
stage ... talking to some magical people ... and seeing
this amazing performance art ... then in the mist of
the music and the night ... the message came from the
singer on the stage ... "anything is possible."

Or . . .

"I met my best friends that I never met before ... I feel
so rich. I can't even begin to to describe how much fun
being a Merry Prankster has been! I've met some of the
Greatest People that I would have never known — all
by taking a chance this summer. I have over 100 New
Friends (and some I'm still meeting) from all over the
country."

Or then . . . Original Bus Prankster Anonymous saying .
. . "You have no idea ... I'm already rebelling and having
thoughts of cross-country driving ... the wonderful thing
is you awoke this sleeper ... and nothing is the same
anymore ...."

It was three days ... but really it was five ... or two weeks
for some ... or six months for a few ... and lifetime for
all. Leading to this place.

Like ... up on the hill, a giant 15 foot high top hat ...
and if you cracked the hidden slit in the side — there
was a full Mad Hatter's tea party going on inside with
china teapots and teacups and a full compliment of Mad

Hatters sitting around speaking Jabberwocky.

Or there's Grandma Tigger baking cookies by day and
blowing fire by night. Or there's the kids painting
their faces and putting on a play on the main stage. Or
there's Anonymous who jumped on The Bus in Calgary
in '64 holding court with tales of The Road. Or there's
me on stage *reading On The Road* with the Adam's
Ale soul-swingers, or my own Road Tales with JoJo
Stella gettin' stellar with the groove. Or there's Aretha's
trombone player blowin' his rhythmic squonks across
the land, saying, "You made lightning strike."

Pranksters. Nuthin but Pranksters. And they're
nuts! You know the type. A little too crazy to fit
in naturally with regular folk … they're always on
Adventures … and playing … and goofing … and smiling
… and hugging. And man! … a first-thought best-
thought was to add up how many miles each person
travelled to be here. Could you imagine?! East Coast,
West Coast, Gulf Coast, Canada … then you know the
way sports are covered? — with every hit & shot &
everything counted? — what if you counted all the hugs
n kisses over this weekend?! We'd be burying Babe
Ruth numbers.

Maybe a lot of groups feel this ... and I've been in some pretty huggy close families ... from Landmark Forum to MTV Networks to Deadheads United ... but there was an inhibition-free love here I haven't experienced before. Cool as the best work family collectives may be, you're prolly not the You you are on a secret weekend getaway. Or in those self-help groups, you have to buy your way into their advanced programs before you're in a really special place. But being a Prankster costs nothing. You don't even have to *like the Dead* — although pretty much everybody does.

It's a mindset. It's about being playful and participatory. Maybe you'd find this in a cool theater company's get-together. Or an invitation-only musicians party. And oh my gawd — the music!

Part of host Wiz's whole idea, which he worked up with Yoda, was that all the musicians would play together. He hired four killer bands of the kinda players you could listen to all night ... and that's just what the hell happened. Saturday there was no break in the music from 8PM till 5 in the morning. A non-stop improvised amalgam of jazz-level cats merging in and out of the flow for nine hours. It was musical medicine alright ... just as Yoda prophesied. And meanwhile on the hillside next to the stage there's a dancing psychedelic light show playing out among the trees as people dance in it and dogs run through chasing the lights causing wolfian sculptures of shadows dancing to the *Fire On The Mountain*. And then a giant octopus appears . . .

And then there's this part where everybody paints or performs or pranks or cooks or makes installations or photographs or cleans up ... or all of the above ... and it's this communal gathering with not just people being nice to each other, but everybody letting their freak flag fly and creating whatever it is they do. Maybe that's playing with somebody and tweakin' their Twanger. Maybe that's bringing 50,000 beers and giving them away like Gubba, Uncle Mike and Hootie did — after flying in from Vancouver and Albuquerque. Or maybe it's tracking down one of the original Bus travelers and flying her in like Moray, the laugh-after-every-line Babbs of the Next Generation, did. Or maybe it's arriving with a half dozen costumes for a three day party. Or maybe it's becoming a Butterfly and dance-flying all around the garden.

Brian Hassett

Whatever it is — everybody brings it.

And the whole gall-darn point is — it can be done anywhere, by anyone. It's just upping your Prankster game, and beaming in on those who shine. Weir everywhere.

But of course *this one* was silly special. The first Family Reunion after the 50th anniversary Bus Tour last year (2014) that brought all the Pranksters out of the woodwork. And now with The Summer of The Dead ... and everything going on in Chicago in July ... this is obviously a springtime to feel free to freak freely — "Let your freak flag fly," as Crosby put it — letting out whatever's inside that wants to emerge. That's the Prankster ethos.

As I talked to people all weekend, from kids to old folks, there was a leprechaun glisten in their eyes, an electric wildtude, a Prankster twinkle. Nobody here was normal. Everyone was touched and screwy in their own way. Didn't fit in. Reminds me of a line in *The Hitchhiker's Guide to Jack Kerouac* about Jack's friends being odd ducks. I dunno, but it worked for him, and it's working for me. The weirdest and most twinklingly playful people around you are prolly the ones you wanna get closest to.

11

The George &
Brian Story

George Walker & I first met in Boulder, Colorado, in July 1982 at the historic Jack Kerouac *On The Road* 25th Anniversary Conference — including when I ran the projector for their multimedia "Cassady" show — and then we hung again the following month at Ken Kesey's home in Pleasant Hill, Oregon.

Flash-forward to 2015 and George is given a copy of my *Hitchhiker's Guide to Jack Kerouac* (about that very summit in Boulder!) by Jami Cassady (Neal & Carolyn's daughter) and "read it cover-to-cover as soon as I got it – and loved every minute of it!"

This led him to read numerous other Beat and Prankster stories on my website (BrianHassett.com), prompting him to write, "I often wonder why I go on this damn thing [the internet] and then every once-in-a-while I find something like this!"

The following summer of 2016 we met up for the first time in 34 years on the tour for the *"Going Furthur"* film we both appeared in.

George was holding court with a half-dozen people behind the theater — and when I first walked up after all these years, he blurted out to his crowd, "Now here's somebody *I* look up to!"

One movie screening led to another, and the next thing you know we're at Alex & Allyson Grey's Church of Sacred Mirrors (COSM) and all that goes with it.

We next found ourselves together at the Merry Prankster / Twanger Plunker Family Reunion in May 2017 where I opened the weekend festivities with a spoken word / theater performance, after which George blurted in bug-eyed amazement — "I'd never seen you on a stage before! That was unbelievable, man!"

That afternoon, hanging in our mutual friend Spirit's trailer, with George still gushing about the show, I said, knowing his close friendship with Neal Cassady, "We should do something together. You read Neal and I'll read Jack. We could do that 'IT' part from *On The Road* where they're sitting in the backseat talking like crazy," and his face was bouncing up and down, "Yes Yes Yes!"

The next day, 15 minutes before the show, George

read that part of *On The Road* for the first time in 30 years . . . and *was* Neal from the opening line of a cold read-through.

He'd first spontaneously channeled his good friend Cassady back in 1973, reading him aloud at fellow Kesey/Cassady pal Ed McClanahan's house, whereupon everyone stopped what they were doing and listened to their old friend appear in the room. George says he's been trying to find a way to bring Cassady to life on a stage ever since.

I've been riffing and performing Kerouac since at least 1994 when I started producing, hosting and performing in a series of Kerouac-inspired shows in Manhattan, L.A., Amsterdam, London, Toronto and elsewhere. Although duetting with countless others over decades of shows, I'd never had a stage partner until now. The duo's flourished because it was loving magic from the first moment we got near microphones.

Since the Prankster Family Reunion performance had gone so well, and I was already booked to do my "Beat Café" show at the world-famous Beat Museum in North Beach San Francisco on Friday June 2nd to kick off the 50th anniversary of the Summer of Love, that became the first full Hassett–Walker show.

The appearance brought more people into The Beat Museum than any event they've ever put on in their history (other than a memorial for a fallen giant). And for the first time, the duo improvised on stage in character as Jack & Neal. The show killed.

I was also booked at the landmark Tsunami Books in hometown Prankster headquarters Eugene Oregon, which then became the second duo show.

Mountain Girl introduced us . . . with her daughter Sunshine Kesey and Ken Babbs in the audience laughing and clapping, the show prompting Tsunami owner Scott Landfield to blurt out, "You just held that audience entranced for two hours. That doesn't happen. You can't do that with just spoken word."

Which prompted us to book a Portland show, and with a week's notice, packed the classic Kerouacian American roadhouse, The Rosebud Cafe, which turned out to be the real birth of the duo. For the first time, in a venue far far away, we both found our voice and rhythm on a whole 'nuthur level.

The show killed. Which segued into the climax of the West Coast Summer of Love Tour in the home of the very first Acid Test — Santa Cruz.

It was set up by the Santa Cruz District Supervisor John Leopold — the same guy who produced the 50th anniversary Acid Test reunion there in 2015 — and his essential gets-things-done point-person Angela Chesnut — and we were joined on stage by Neal & Carolyn's only son John Allen Cassady and their daughter Jami. The show killed — prompting Lance Simmens to write about it in the *Huffington Post*.

Then we went and filmed the "IT" scene in the back of the '49 Hudson (that was used in the movie *On The Road*) at The Beat Museum . . .

. . . then over to the Cassady's old house at 29 Russell St. where the classic Jack & Neal shot was taken by Carolyn Cassady in 1952 . . . then out to touch base with The Bus that started it all . . . The Most Famous Bus in America, according to *Time* magazine.

And while all this was happening, bookings started to come in for festivals and clubs and music halls and acid tests all over the continent — as it also kicked in that we were performing a book that was having its 60th anniversary of being in print.

Onward and Furthur forever!

The original 1939 International Harvester ... with the original driver/mechanic.

147

12

Keeping the Beat:
A brief personal history of how the Beats begat the Merry Pranksters

by George Walker

"Keeping the Beat, boys, frees my soul . . ."; not to get lost in rock and roll, but the music has always been a part of it — from jazz greats Lester Young and Coleman Hawkins (among Cassady's favorites), through be-bop's Diz & Bird (Dizzy Gillespie & Charlie Parker), Coltrane & Miles Davis, and Dave Brubeck's milestone *Time Out*, to the Beatles and the Grateful Dead.

Kerouac's many references and descriptions of the various jazz events he and his friends dug in *On The Road*, John Clellon Holmes' beautiful, evocative novel *The Horn*, and the live collaborations of Kerouac and other Beat poets with jazz musicians such as David Amram set the stage for what was considered cool in the 1950s, and led to that wonderful time now called, simply, The Sixties, when we saw Allen Ginsberg with Bob Dylan.

Picking up on both the music and the style of the Beats,

in 1960 Mike Hagen opened a coffee house/jazz joint he called "The Abyss" in the basement of an old house on the University of Oregon campus in Eugene. I was friends with Mike, and hung out there, learning in upstairs rooms to smoke weed and hearing his intriguing stories about his great friend Ken Kesey, now living on Perry Lane in Palo Alto and embracing the new hipness. I became determined to meet him, and when he showed up with Perry Lane friends Roy Sebern and Carl Lehmann-Haupt I realized that goal, and began friendships that have lasted a lifetime.

Those of us who became known as the Merry Pranksters had read *On The Road,* and, like many others were to a considerable degree, affected by it. The America in which we grew up during and after World War II, was in a state of flux, its rapid changes both encouraging and restricting freedom of thought and action, and Kerouac's ground-breaking work helped to provide a road map with which to navigate the often turbulent waters of social change. Magazine and newspaper articles about "Beats" and even "beatniks" served to blaze the trail to the cool places we would soon seek.

We learned to laugh at such feeble attempts of the established order to constrain us such as *Reefer Madness*, and when Robert Mitchum was sent to prison for marijuana possession in 1948 it stimulated curiosity rather than fear or loathing. Thus, the stage was set when, one day in the early sixties, Neal Cassady, the model for "Dean Moriarty" in *On The Road*, pulled up in the driveway of Ken Kesey's house in longtime Bohemian enclave known as Perry Lane, a few blocks from the VA hospital where Kesey had participated in government-sponsored psychoactive drug experiments that led to his writing of his equally ground-breaking novel, *One Flew Over The Cuckoo's Nest.*

It was, for me at least, Cassady's entrance into the scene that really made the connection to the Beats. I had read *On The Road* in 1958, the year after it was published, at the insistence of my freshman English Composition teacher at the University of Oregon, and was initially only mildly affected by it. Afflicted at an early age by a rather high degree of telepathic awareness, I was interested in elevated states of consciousness, although I wouldn't then have referred to it as such. The growing media coverage of the increasing experiments with mind-altering substances such as LSD and psilocybin seemed to fit right in with Kerouac's frequent references to the use of drugs, mainly marijuana and amphetamines, in seeking a satisfying life free of the societal constraints that seemed to dictate a conforming, soul-cramped life style. The prospects of that life seemed rather dreary — and I was ready for something different.

I wasn't there the day Neal first showed up at Kesey's, but met him at another friend's house a few months later. At first, I didn't take to him. His seemingly excessive exuberance, exemplified by his boundless kinetic energy and endless fast-talking manner by which he expounded on a vast variety of subjects, and even (it seemed to me) on no subject at all, of which I could make little or no sense, was off-putting. In short, I thought he was uncool. I thought of cool people as constrained, rather quiet, calm, in control. Neal Cassady was none of that. He was, however, Dean Moriarty, *that guy,* and thus worthy of note.

And so it came to pass, in the ensuing weeks and months, I saw more and more of him. He began to come visit me at my house a few blocks from Perry Lane (I usually had some pot to smoke), and I learned to listen to him as he expounded on subjects that were quite foreign to me, such as "karma" (a word I had never heard, much less understood), and reincarnation. He'd had "life readings," and referred frequently to his "karma tapes," which detailed his past lives, and extolled the work of the famous mystic Edgar Cayce. In a single seemingly endless sentence he might reference his vast knowledge of literature, history, politics, or metaphysical philosophy, mixed with his own ever-shifting viewpoint on any or all of these subjects, and how they might somehow relate to the present moment.

It wasn't easy listening to Neal, as the real "meat" of his conversation was constantly conflated with obfuscation, denial, reversals of position, subject matter shifting faster than Sahara sands, intertwining a vast array of seemingly unrelated subjects, and all manner of quirky styles of delivery that could confuse the quickest of minds, all delivered at breathtaking speed.

As difficult as it was, I slowly came to know and understand him, and Neal and I became close friends. I came to appreciate his enthusiasm for life and all it could entail, and thus altered my perception of what could be considered "cool." It didn't hurt our relationship that we shared a high level of interest in motor racing, and fast cars in general. He began calling me "Cousin George." "If you can't beat 'em, join 'em!" he would say, referring to my regular victories in our clandestine races, doubtless due to my vastly superior car, and little to do with skill, as nobody could drive like Neal. And few dared try.

A year or so after meeting Neal, I became friends with another artist of that generation, the late and virtually unknown/forgotten Big Sur sculptor Ron Boise, notable if for nothing else than being unsuccessfully prosecuted for obscenity (think Ginsberg's *Howl*) for his Kama Sutra-themed metal sculptures exhibited at Vorpal Gallery in San Francisco. Boise would probably not be considered a part of the "Beat Generation," as such, not being a verbal artist like most of the others, but his work and lifestyle exemplified the spirit of the movement.

He became an important influence on me, as he moved his truck (in which he lived with his stunningly beautiful Spanish mistress/model/inspiration) into my back yard in Berkeley, and I helped him assemble the aforementioned show for a couple of weeks, with a trip or two to La Honda to meet Kesey & the Pranksters. From then until his untimely death in 1966, he played a prominent part in our activities.

When Neal blew up two engines in two weeks in the car I gave him in 1966 (the same 1958 Chevy Yeoman station wagon that Ken & I, with Sandy Lehmann-Haupt, drove back to Oregon in the fall of 1963, after regaling ourselves at the Broadway opening of Dale Wasserman's stage adaptation of *One Flew Over The Cuckoo's Nest*) I took back the car and gave it to Ron to turn into sculpture, as he was doing large pieces such as Kesey's original "Thunder Machine," a prominent fixture at the parties in La Honda that morphed into the Acid Tests. Later, when Kesey fled in exile to Mexico, it was Ron Boise who drove him to Puerto Vallarta, a destination for Neal and me a year later.

In the spring of 1964 Kesey bought the "Furthur" bus for $1,500. His second novel, *Sometimes a Great Notion*, was being published by Viking Press, and we, the Merry Band of Pranksters, were taking Furthur to New York for the publication event and party, and to attend the New York World's Fair. In preparation for the trip, I had gone to see my ex-roommate in Berkeley, anonymously known herein as "Mr. Big" (he was actually a *very* small-time drug dealer, an occasional lid of pot or hit of LSD), who had connected with Dr. Timothy Leary in the days when Tim was turning on the world, and I procured a few dozen sugar-cubes loaded with acid.

A couple of weeks before departure, the Pranksters gathered at Kesey's home in La Honda, consumed a few of said sugar-cubes, and on a warm, sunny Sunday proceeded to paint Furthur with all the paint we could find, in as many patterns as we could create, with the guidance of our best artist/painter Roy Sebern (who also named her Furthur that day), to the wailing strains of John Coltrane's "*Africa/Brass*," Mike Hagen filming the events with his newly acquired pawnshop Bolex 16mm and a dozen or so rolls of Kodachrome.

The days following were consumed with preparations for the trip. Quite a few of our friends came by La Honda to check out the progress, Cassady often among them, frequently showing up in his beat old car, at that time a red Plymouth of obscure origin and vintage, with his oft-changing posse of misfits, mistresses, followers and flacks, as well as a few near-genius oddballs, all of whom I suspect he terrorized with his madcap drives over the twists and turns of La Honda Road, aka Highway 84.

As the departure day approached, Cassady's visits became more frequent, his interest more intense. Then, two or three days before we were ready to roll, Neal came by and announced to us that he would be driving the bus to New York. "Got to take care of you kids," is how he put it.

The next day, he showed up with all his tire-changing gear: ten-ton hydraulic jack, heavy-duty Budd-wheel lug wrench, two-ended to fit the dual rear wheels, a bar that doubled as both a handle for the lug wrench and a pry-bar to free tires from rims, and a special tire hammer to break down the heavy tires from the wheel rims (long-handled, not the little 3-pound sledge made famous by Tom Wolfe's description of Neal's constant throw-and-catch in *The Electric Kool-Aid Acid Test*). He also brought a spare inner tube (no tubeless tires back in the day), and a spare "flap," a large rubber band that fits between the inner tube and the steel wheel to prevent chafing.

It turned out to be a good idea; we were only about three days out when we had our first flat tire, which was not to be the last! By the time we returned from Mexico, two years later, he had replaced every tire (always with used tires from some junk pile or other), some of them more than once. Remarkably, after all these years, the last tires Neal installed (in 1966!) are still holding air.

Dubbed "Sir Speed Limit" by Kesey after a night of unusually spectacular driving of Furthur through the Blue

Ridge Mountains of the Carolinas and Virginia, Neal, Furthur, and the Merry Pranksters were cemented in fact and legend.

After many weeks of circling North America in Furthur, Kesey and the Pranksters settled in and around La Honda. Frequent parties and gatherings ensued, including several visits by the Hells Angels, and various semi-illustrious individuals who were prominent in the burgeoning drug culture.

Among the visitors was Allen Ginsberg, the already-legendary Beat poet, who became a good friend to Kesey and the Pranksters, and helped solidify the connection between the Beat Generation and the hippies and Merry Pranksters. When the Angels threatened to disrupt a Vietnam War protest in Oakland, Kesey and the Pranksters drove Furthur to Oakland, with Cassady at the wheel, to defuse the situation. That evening found Kesey, Cassady, Babbs, and Ginsberg at the home of Hells Angels President Sonny Barger, smoking peace pipes, and Ginsberg, short, balding, Jewish, and queer, sitting on the floor chanting "ommmm" and keeping time with tiny brass Buddhist finger cymbals from India. There was no violence that day.

Through the summer of 1965 the Saturday parties at La Honda continued, with various luminaries connected to the Beat and Psychedelic movements showing up, including Cassady, Ginsberg, Gerd Stern, Richard Alpert (later Ram Dass), Jim Fadiman, Stewart Brand, and many others. It became a virtual melting pot for the various factions of what became nothing short of a consciousness revolution.

It was an exhilarating time. But it quickly became apparent that we were attracting too much attention, so Kesey announced that we would begin holding our events in different locations. They would be called "Acid Tests." An advertising flyer was drawn: "Can You Pass the Acid Test?" I acquired a significant supply of LSD, which was supplied to attendees (and ourselves) in (usually) small doses, and a band known as the Warlocks was engaged to provide entertainment. They soon became the Grateful Dead, about whom much has been written, and who were also heavily influenced in early life by Kerouac and the Beats. With Cassady present at all these events, and the states of mind so elevated, it was inevitable that Neal would astound and impress Garcia and his bandmates as he had so many others before, and his exploits were further immortalized in many of their songs.

"A Prankster, a Warlock, and a Beatnik walk into a bar ..."

Twice busted for pot possession, Kesey withdrew to Mexico in the winter of 1966. After a few more months of holding Acid Tests in and around Los Angeles, the Pranksters followed him, driving in Furthur to Mazatlan and a planned meeting, then on to Manzanillo, a bustling west-coast shipping port that saw few tourists, where we took up residence for several months.

When we left California to meet up with Kesey (and Hagen and Zonker who had joined him earlier), we did not bring Neal. Before long, we realized the error in this, and I was dispatched to California to find him, and bring him to join us. After an eventful trip in Neal's car at the time, a red 1955 Chrysler with a hemi engine and barely any brakes, we arrived at our "casa grande" in Manzanillo. Neal stayed with us for the rest of our stay, eventually driving Furthur to Mexico City, over the mountains to the Gulf Coast during a hurricane, and back to California in time for the Acid Test Graduation, on Halloween, 1966. By then he was a member of the family, and an inspiration for the Pranksters as much as he had been for the Beats half a generation earlier.

The final chapter of our relationship came the following year, when Neal and I, along with his then-girlfriend Anne Murphy, and Steve "Zonker" Lambrecht, & his then-girlfriend Gloria (later) Quarnstrom, drove to Puerto Vallarta for the winter, in my day-glo painted Lotus sports car and a 1960 Ford that Zonker borrowed from his parents and which Neal would kill on a trip to Guadalajara. After many adventures, to be chronicled in detail at a later date, Neal and I were driving south from Guadalajara, to reconnect with Zonker (in a different car) in Oaxaca, but mechanical problems dictated otherwise, and, seeking refuge at near-dark, with no lights, we landed in San Miguel de Allende where we knew people. That turned out to be a fateful decision, as Neal made connections there that led him to return, and on one of those trips he died, less than a year later, on February 4, 1968.

Now, nearly half a century later, Neal's continuing influence on all who knew him cannot be overstated. Without Neal, our driver, teacher, friend, and sometimes guru, the Merry Pranksters would not be the same. He brought the spirit that inspired the Beat Generation and hugely influenced the writing of Kerouac and others, works that are the very roots of all that our movement has become: Pranksters, Deadheads, hippies, and even now, the several groups around the country that are carrying on the consciousness-raising work of the Merry Pranksters.

13

I Pick *Pic*

Thirty years ago I remember saying to my Beat brothers at the Cedar Tavern in Greenwich Village that I thought *Vanity of Duluoz* was right up there with Jack's greatest works. And they all looked at me like I was crazy, saying, "Yeah, but nobody else thinks that."

Years later, *Duluoz* has gotten its due.

What I'm sayin here is — Jack Kerouac's *Pic* is better than conventional wisdom has it.

If you don't know — this novella was a key moment in the evolution of one of America's greatest writers. It was written over the summer / fall of 1950 as he was struggling to get his *On The Road* vision on the page.

Shortly after writing it, in Dec. 1950 he received the now-legendary "Joan Anderson/Cherry Mary letter" from Neal Cassady that broke open his storytelling narrative voice which led to the famous Scroll version three months later.

I know it sounds crazy, but I think the oft-dismissed *Pic* is one of Kerouac's most fun (and quick) books. Everything Jack wrote was a thinly-veiled version of himself. This is the only time he ever wrote as someone else entirely — a precocious, adorable, funny, adventurous, wide-eyed 10-year-old African-American boy from North Carolina.

His whole oeuvre, his whole raison d'êtra, his whole "Duluoz Legend" (the breakthrough idea of telling one epic story of one person's life at his particular point in history) was about writing in the real first person. *Pic* is Kerouac's very first work written in first-person (after the third-person *Town and The City, Orpheus Emerged, The Sea Is My Brother*, et al) and the only book to step into another skin entirely — a key evolution in the author's expanding execution.

I'm not saying *Pic* is *Road* — but it does contain many scenes he either used (in a different form) in *On The Road* or in the Scroll version or elsewhere that never stayed in the published editions. There's the longest take of the Ghost of the Susquehanna; there's the Prophet of Times Square and other vivid New York scenes; there's the most detailed bus trip description of his many times riding in one; and there's the whole story of two "brothers" going "on the road" together.

This is the only time this stunningly gifted writer ever branched into a wholly other voice. And boy, I love it!

And just to clarify the "stunningly gifted writer" part if anybody doesn't get it, and I know some don't:

What I might suggest anyone do is read the *On The Road Scroll* and *Old Angel Midnight* and *The Dharma Bums* and *Big Sur* and get back to me. Kerouac captured a compassionate vision of the world, and an embrace of all peoples — black, white; gay, straight;

160

rich, poor; city hipsters and country farmers. He
articulated the wanderlust that so many have, whether
they act on it or not. He wrote prose like a poet, and
novels like a storyteller sitting next to you in a bar (as he
himself described his goal as a writer).

His output was a herculean effort in a very short
47-year life that was filled — except for about one week

in 1957 — with mostly rejection. There's a body of work
here that's rivaled only by his fellow giants. Besides
being a novelist, he was a chronicler, an historian, a poet
— a visionary in the sense that he saw the future and
knew the value of what he was doing — and that people
are still devouring what he created is proof he was
right. As of 2017, he has over 50 books in print. And I
mean — *you're reading about him now!*

It was a Van Gogh-like commitment in the face of all rejection. And God-damn-it that hard booze and insulting dismissals mowed him down in mid-life.

And in his whole massive masterful output, *Pic* has not gotten the props it deserves — just like John Lennon's *"Sometime In New York City"* album didn't. As a Lennon fan, I was always perplexed by the accepted conclusion that this album was no good. I had it. I listened to it. I knew it was great. In fact, it rocked!

And so, like everybody else in Jackland, I'd dismissed *Pic* (until I reread it recently) because ... *it was dismissed.* It's barely touched on in any of the biographies. Sure, it's unfinished, sure the dialect may not be a perfect linguistic transcription, but this is his *Catcher*, his *Huck* — his comical, colorful young-person's voice and story.

I've said (as I'm sure others have) that *On The Road* was *Huckleberry Finn* in the 20th century. In fact, even Jack described this early attempt at *Road* as, "a kind of *Huckleberry Finn* of today." Only thing is — *Huck* was written in dialect, and *Road* wasn't.

This is the only time this monster talent tried a long-form dialect piece. Besides the *Midnight / Sax / Vanity* variety of voices he captured . . . here he is a thousand miles out of his comfort zone — not writing in his native French, nor his mastered English, but actually "becoming" the black American he confessed to wanting to be in *On The Road* — "At lilac evening I walked with every muscle aching among the lights of 27th and Welton in the Denver colored section, wishing I were a Negro, feeling that the best the white world had offered was not enough ecstasy for me, not enough life, joy, kicks, darkness, music, not enough night."

And there's this neat symmetry how this first first-person novel perfectly mirrors the last one he wrote

(*Vanity of Duluoz*) in that they're the only two books addressed throughout to one person — *Pic* to "Grandpa" and *Vanity* to "Wifey" — the most direct one-to-one communication from author to imagined reader.

I'm not sayin *Pic* is Toni Morrison or James Baldwin or Langston Hughes — but I've never read Norman Mailer or Tom Wolfe or Hunter Thompson even attempt this kind of range.

It's a testimony to his creative courage and ear-to-hand gifts that he went there long-form — that he inhabited this other place. Whether he caught every phrase just right, I don't know or care. I "got" it. I was there with him. I was that kid. Going On The Road. Discovering New York. Digging the Ghost of the Susquehanna. Savoring all of America that he was gulping in for the first time. Appreciating how this was Jack's *Road* vision . . . just before he Scrolled it.

And he had (wisely?) returned to it in the last months of his life — dashing off a quick ending that doesn't satisfy but at least didn't leave it mid-tale.

Which brings us back the goddamned tragedy of him dying. Alcoholism is as much a biological disease as cancer. I'm so sad John Lennon was taken from us by another's mental disease, and Jack by his own physical one.

Where would he have gone as an author?

I like to think *Pic* was a hint of one of the places this master storyteller might have taken his readers in the decades he and the rest of us were robbed of.

14

Be the Invincible
Spirit You Are

Lights dimmed, room hushed, MC in silhouette at
center stage blessing the packed room of book-reading
edge-cutting hipsters from all over the world, thanks
to email and websites and a collective unconscious that
keeps them striving for the new, for where the heart
pounds, the eyes twinkle, the women aren't treated like
girls, and the men have self-confidence without conceit.
The lively linguist at the microphone calls up . . . John
Cassady — son-of-a Beat, Neal, icon of time — his nearly
white faded jeans matching his white halo hair, who
begins to spin a web of the road, of wanderlust, soul-
searching, pine-climbing, spine-needling pursuits of
what's through the next door, who's at the next table,
and when's the next epiphany drifting away in the eyes
of another as everything dissolves into a candlelit dream
of two people's faces. Then Breath Cox comes up, down
from Cherry Valley, trim and straight-legged in cowboy
confidence reading classic couplets in a sensuous, lip-
curling elegance that stops even the waitresses in their

rounds, the poetry attenuating the vibe and vibrating the antennas until every head is quivering. Dancing butterfly imagery spins from the lips all night, the room's transformed, the dream's alive. A band starts up, subtle at first, then two dancers on stage, and the Beat's jamming jazzman David Amram is massaging the grand, with saxophone shades weaving in from the corners, and the brick wall backdrop dancing with shadows of clarinet solos, as more cats stream into the scene and fall into the jam — the djembe, the congas, the violin and the bow. A poet, a prankster, a king and a queen. A flirt, a chat, you know what I mean. On your feet dancing, warmed by the light of a new beam beside you, dancing off demons with a smile inside you, dancing with purpose in a circle of light, in a bass-thumping heart-pounding soul-swirling twirl, to dance above the diamond earth, to stoke the improbable, light the impossible, fan the invisible, be in the invincible spirit you are.

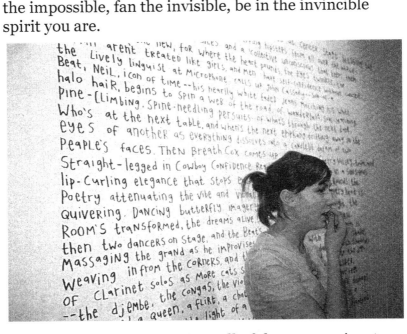

The piece painted onto the wall of the Artomatic+ Art Gallery in London

Brian Hassett

Forever

going

Furthur

with

the

mad ones

167

Photo Credits

Front cover — by author (in Boulder '82)

Back cover — backdrop — Sky Lyons' tie-dye
Center photo of Brandon Loberg's Beat Café poster — by author
Bus at Yasgur's farm — by Angie Lee
George & author at The Beat Museum — by Dale "Gubba" Topham
Carolyn Cassady & Ken Babbs at Boulder '82 — unknown
Author & Sky at Kesey's Bus — by Dale "Gubba" Topham
Author & George at original Furthur — by Sky Lyons
Author at Adventure Travel Office — unknown
Author, Walter Salles & Jim Canary in Bloomington — unknown
Anonymous & Big Al Hinkle at The Beat Museum — by author
Author, Phil Lesh & George Walker at Terrapin Crossroads — by Randy Turley

Allen Ginsberg & Ken Kesey on stage (p. 3) — unknown

Carolyn & Babbs (p. 9) — unknown
Levi Asher, Anonymous, Al Hinkle & Tom Lake (p. 19) — by author
Kesey and author (p. 21) — by Allen Ginsberg
The Wizard of Wonder & David Amram (p. 27) — by Philip Thomas
Author, Al Hinkle & Jami Cassady (p. 30) — by Dawn Hinkle
Author & comedian Will Durst (p. 33) — unknown
Gerd Stern & author on Vallejo (p. 35) — unknown
Jami Cassady pointing at photo on stage (p. 35) — unknown
Amram, Jami, Al Hinkle, Levi & author (p. 38) — unknown
Group shot at Beat Shindig (p. 40) — unknown
Group shot at Vesuvio's (p. 44) — unknown
Author at Adventure Travel Office (p. 45) — unknown
Coit Tower at sunrise (p. 51) — by author
Columbus Tower (Zoetrope) & Transamerica Pyramid (p. 51) — by author
Phil Lesh and author (p. 59) — by Cliff
Author on Halloween 1980 (p. 61) — by Brother Tom
Kesey and author (p. 68) — by Allen Ginsberg
Author at empty Somerset House courtyard (p. 71) — unknown
Author at Somerset House movie screen (p. 73) — unknown
Author with actor Danny Morgan (p. 74) — by Noemie Sornet
Bed set-up at Somerset House (p. 75) — by author
Waterloo Station sign & statue (p. 77) — by author
Author at Somerset House (p. 79) — by Noemie Sornet
Kristen Stewart (p. 82) — by author
Walter Salles on stage (p. 84) — by author
Garrett Hedlund (p. 85) — by author
On The Road cast on stage (p. 87) — by author
Damo, Walter Salles & author (p. 92) — unknown
Walter Salles & author (p. 99) — by Damian D'Aguilar
Author & Walter Salles (p. 103) — unknown
Author and resident of 454 West 20th St. (p. 110) — by Debbie Vazquez
Regina Weinreich & Ann Charters (p. 112) — by author
Kristen Stewart signature (p. 114) — by author
Walter Salles & Patti Smith (p. 116) — by author
Author & Debbie Vazquez (p. 117) — unknown

Author at Yasgur's farm historical marker (p. 122) — unknown

Author inside Kesey's Bus at Kerouac image (p. 123) — by Milton Rosenberg

Group shot outside Kesey Bus (p. 125) — unknown

Kesey Bus at Yasgur's barn (p. 128) — by Angie Lee

Pranksters jumping at sunset (p. 131) — unknown

Furthur sign on Bus (p. 133) — by author

Grandma Tigger, Moray & Spirit Mentalist (p. 136) — by author

Author on stage with Jojo Stella (p. 138) — by Dale "Gubba" Topham

Author, Wizard of Wonder, Jim Canary (p. 139) — by Jeremy Hogan

Butterfly (p. 140) — by Dale "Gubba" Topham

Wizard of Wonder (p. 141) — unknown

Prankster group shot (p. 142) — Jeremy Hogan

Pranksters at CoSM (p. 144) — unknown

George Walker & author at The Beat Museum (p. 145) — by Dale Topham

George Walker & author at the '49 Hudson (p. 147) — by David Stewart

Author & George Walker at original Furthur (p. 147) — by Sky Lyons

Author, Phil Lesh & George Walker (p. 156) — by Randy Turley

Pic book cover (p. 161) — by author

London art gallery wall (p. 166) — unknown

Made in the USA
San Bernardino, CA
18 December 2017